# Shortcuts to Success

## English Essay Writing
### Leaving Certificate Higher Level

Martin Kieran and Frances Rocks

Gill & Macmillan

Gill & Macmillan Ltd
Hume Avenue
Park West
Dublin 12

with associated companies throughout the world www.gillmacmillan.ie

© Martin Kieran and Frances Rocks 2005

0 7171 3831 3

Colour reproduction and print origination in Ireland by Metaphor

The paper used in this book is made from the wood pulp of managed forests.
For every tree felled, at least one tree is planted, thereby renewing natural resources.

# CONTENTS

# INTRODUCTION

essay *n* 1. literary composition 2. an organised collection of ideas

For Paper 1 of the Leaving Certificate English examination (Higher Level), students are asked to write about a wide variety of subjects. The Composing section also includes short stories. Three lengthy literary essays must be written in Paper 2.

**English Essay Writing:**

- teaches the **technique** of studying the wording of questions, identifying the task, and arranging notes and points into successful answers
- includes many **examples** of Leaving Cert answers in all sections of the papers to show students how to raise C-Grade work to A-Grade standard
- provides **essay assignments** and shorter **tasks** in effective writing – planning and organising points, paragraphing, openings, good description, conclusions, developing writing skills, etc.
- deals with other types of essay writing, e.g. **Comprehending B questions,** including various functional writing styles, such as diary-writing, letters, advertising, speeches, radio talks, interviews, etc.

The basic skills of a **first-class literature essay** are also covered, including:

- what makes a very good Single Text answer in fiction and drama
- writing excellent Comparative Study essays
- effective responses to Poetry.

**Guidelines and samples** (plus useful Examiner's Comments) are given throughout.

## Writing A-Grade Essays

This book is designed to answer the question: 'How do I write a **top-grade essay** in the Leaving Certificate English Higher Level course?'

Students always ask:

- *How should I approach the question?*

  Methods are suggested to help the student to focus clearly on a close reading of the exam question.

- *What points should I include? How long should the answer be?*

  Students are taught to brainstorm and organise a useful answer plan.
  Clear guidelines are given about the length of answers.

- *What evidence or illustrations are needed?*

  The use of examples and succinct quotation is explored. Guidelines are given on expanding the discussion of relevant points within the given time frame. The student is shown the technique of paragraph writing.

- *How do I start? How do I write a strong ending?*

  Practice is given in writing effective openings and conclusions.

- *How are essays marked?*

  The PCLM marking scheme used in the Leaving Certificate Examination is explained in full. (See page 7.)

# Why is Essay Writing so Important?

Another question frequently asked is: 'Where exactly on the paper do I have to write an essay?'

**Essay-style answers are required throughout both papers and account for 330 marks out of 400 (or 83% of the total).**

Students must write successful essays in:

- Comprehending (Paper 1, Section 1B): **50 marks**
- Composing (Paper 1, Section 2): **100 marks**
- Single Text (Paper 2, Section 1): **60 marks**
- Comparative Study (Paper 2, Section 2): **70 marks**
- Prescribed Poetry (Paper 2, Section 3): **50 marks**

These are the challenges facing students sitting the Higher Level English Examination. If you prepare well, use your imagination and express yourself clearly, you can achieve the Leaving Cert grade you want.

This book is aimed at:

- **students** – who need revision and up-to-the-minute preparation on the qualities required for writing A-Grade essays
- **teachers** – for regular use in English classes throughout Fifth and Sixth Year
- **parents** – to help them give reassurance in a structured way to students facing one of the most challenging exam papers in the Leaving Certificate.

# The PCLM Marking Scheme

The criteria for assessment for all questions (of 50 marks or more) are as follows:

## Clarity of Purpose (30%)

This refers to 'engagement with the task'. Has the student engaged with the task? Relevance, focus, originality, freshness, clear aim, and understanding of genre are rewarded here.

## Coherence of delivery (30%)

This refers to the 'ability to sustain the response over the entire answer'. Can the candidate keep the logic of the argument going? Continuity of argument, sequencing, management of ideas, choice of reference, use of examples (anecdotes, illustrations), engagement with texts, control of register and shape, and creative modelling are rewarded in this section.

## Efficiency of Language use (30%)

This refers to 'management and control of language to achieve clear communication'. Has the candidate used language suitable for the task? Vocabulary, syntax, sentence patterns, paragraph structure, punctuation appropriate to the register, use of lively and interesting phrasing, energy, style and fluency appropriate to the task are examined here.

## Accuracy of Mechanics (10%)

This refers to 'spelling and grammar'. Appropriate levels of accuracy in spelling, and grammatical patterns appropriate to the register are examined here.

This scheme is usually referred to as the **PCLM**. It is a precise method of marking that rewards students with a fair mark for their efforts.

# SECTION 1
# COMPREHENDING: QUESTION B

The **functional writing** questions in this section ask you to write for a specific purpose. This is examined in the B section of Paper 1. It is worth 50 marks (equal to the marks for the main Prescribed Poetry question).

It is marked in accordance with the grid PCLM: 15, 15, 15 and 5. Questions usually take the form of a newspaper account, diary entries, a radio talk, review, speech, letter, interview, advertisement etc.

The **register** is all-important. The piece of writing you do must have the authentic 'feel' of a real news article, diary, talk, etc. So the student must be aware of the form and know his/her audience. It is also important to sustain the response over the whole piece.

Comprehending B answers are meant to be relatively short. The average length is approximately 300–350 words, so work should be focused and concise.

## Planning is Vital

The student must study the wording of the question carefully and consider:

- the task – on what do I have to write? Sort out the content.
- form/genre – what shape should this communication be? Letter, talk, diary entry etc.
- audience – to whom am I speaking/writing?
- persona – who am I as writer?
- register – what kind of words will I choose? Will the tone be formal/informal?

*I can't write without a reader. It's precisely like a kiss ... You can't do it alone.*
John Cheever

## EXAM TIP

Remember to check:

- what do I have to do?
- what shape should this communication be?
- to whom am I writing?
- who am I as the writer?
- register?

**Here is an example of a Comprehending B question.**

You have been asked to give a short radio talk in which you complain about noise pollution in towns and cities.

What do I have to speak about?

Complaints about irritating noise around town.

What shape should this be?

A radio talk.

To whom am I speaking?

An early morning radio audience.

Who am I as speaker?

A 30-something radio journalist.

Register?

Informal, chatty, humorous.

## *TASK*

Write the middle section (about 100–150 words) of the radio talk. The opening and concluding paragraphs are already done for you.

Some of these suggestions might be useful for the middle section:

- Muzak (bland background music heard in public places)
- music on phones when you've been put 'on hold'
- noisy neighbours and their roaring lawnmowers
- rock concerts – decibels
- late-night revellers
- car radios at the seaside – the latest GAA commentary at full volume.

**Opening Paragraph**

Good morning, listeners, and let me take you on a journey of surround sound...

'I Got the Music in Me' blared from the supermarket loudspeakers as I stood in the palace of plenty trying to work out if the price of potatoes had gone up since last week. Did I remember to bring shopping bags, and how many calories extra (and surely didn't I deserve them?) would it add if I made potato gratin rather than boring baked? I didn't want the music in me. I wanted peace and quiet to work all this out.

**Concluding Paragraph**

Fortunately, at the end of a long hard day's work, as all the best modern magazines suggest, it's 'me-time'. I head off for a new course of yoga – deep breathing, a small amount of exercise and tranquillity – just what I need – deep peace! But then the instructor says, 'I have a surprise'. I can feel myself tense. She produces a CD player. 'As you relax, you can listen to the music of the whales from the South Pole.' I wasn't bothering the whales. I had even bought politically correct tuna today. Why did the whales have to sing to me? What a day of surround sound!

# EXAM TIP

**Fluent, legible handwriting** will help to make a positive impression. Corrections should be made neatly (by simply drawing a line through the mistake). Scored-out words distract attention from the content of your work.

Try to develop handwriting that:

- is legible and neat, with words evenly spaced
- is a sensible size – not too large or small, too cramped or spread out
- shapes and joins letters consistently
- leans one way, if it leans at all.

Experiment with styles of writing and different pens so that you can write comfortably, neatly and quickly.

# CHAPTER 1
# SPEAKING OUT!

The task of writing a short talk is a popular Comprehending B question. It is worth spending some time thinking about the context of a particular talk. In some cases, you will be asked to assume a persona and play a particular role.

For example, it may be a radio presenter appealing for a favourite charity, a football manager giving a pep talk to players or a school principal saying goodbye to Sixth Years.

Whatever kind of talk you are giving, you will be rewarded for:

- a clear appreciation of the task
- understanding the audience being addressed
- the consistency of the register adopted.

Imagine that you are the spokesperson for a well-known airline. Write out the text of a talk you would give to passengers whose holiday flight has been delayed for five hours. Explain the reasons for the delay and suggest some ways to help the holidaymakers spend their time at the airport.

## SAMPLE ANSWER

*Good afternoon, ladies and gentlemen. Could I have your attention for a few moments, please? Thank you. My name is Karen Reilly and I am the Customer Relations spokesperson for Euro Air Tours.*

*Firstly, I wish to apologise for the delay of your holiday flight E322 to Malaga. Unfortunately, there has been a terrorist alert at Malaga Airport and security staff there have cancelled all flights while a detailed check is being carried out.*

*I must stress that the delay is due to an alert. We have been advised that the authorities are hoping to get flights back to normal within a matter of hours. Plans are also being made to deal with any backlog by redirecting fights to other airports close to Malaga. We now expect that your flight out of Dublin will leave at approximately 3.45 p.m., which means that you will still be in Spain this evening well before the sun goes down.*

*In the meantime, could I remind you that there are many facilities to avail of here in the airport. In the first-floor food court, Euro Air Tours are now offering a complimentary meal for all passengers due to travel on Flight E322. Adjacent to the main restaurant is the Play Zone, which is suitable for children up to the age of twelve years. The shopping section on the second floor is well worth a look. And I would recommend a visit to the fourth floor viewing area.*

*Once again, ladies and gentlemen, I apologise for the inconvenience caused by this delay and, on behalf of Euro Air Tours, I would like to thank you all for your continuing patience. Although it is particularly difficult for families to have to wait around for so long, I know that you understand the importance of airport safety at this time.*

*I will also be here at the Euro Air Tours desk all afternoon and will be very happy to deal with any particular queries you may have. If we receive any new information, we will let you know as soon as possible. Thank you again for your attention.*

## EXAMINER'S COMMENTS

This is a very well-organised piece of writing, which has the convincing feel of a reassuring talk. The tone is polite and positive, achieving the correct register throughout. The speaker explains the delay in a straightforward way and appeals to the passengers' good sense. Effective use is made of details regarding the flight and airport facilities. A very good A grade standard.

## SAMPLE ANSWER

*Could I have your attention for the Madrid flight from Dublin? On behalf of Certified Flights, I am sorry for your delay. I understand that children are cranky and adults are bored. But due to weather conditions, all planes have been held up. The flight in from Madrid was two and a half hours late. Also, due to the bad flight, there were many sick passengers and the plane will have to be cleaned.*

*Now, to solve the problem of your cranky children, the new Adventurama has opened, so you can get a break from all the kids. Also, we have a big arcade with loads of gaming machines and a pool room for older people. As it is nearly 7.00am, the bars are now open and so are the restaurants. Also, there is the airport shopping area, my own personal favourite. As I speak, there is a really brilliant twenty per cent reduction on all major-selling perfumes.*

*The delay is not the fault of Certified Flights. It is completely out of our control. Also, I can assure you that if you can just wait patiently for a further two or three hours, I can promise you a fun-filled flight.*

## EXAMINER'S COMMENTS

The abrupt tone of this basic D-grade talk could be greatly improved. There is little sense of either regret or sympathy, and the suggestions for passing the time are questionable. Some of the expression is weak and many sentences begin with 'also'. Much more attention should have been given to the task and to the expectations of the audience.

## TASK

Paragraph 2 contains several inappropriate comments. The speaker refers to the 'cranky children' and her personal preference for shopping. Rewrite the paragraph, adopting a polite tone which will reassure the tired passengers.

## CHAPTER 2
# WRITING REPORTS

A report is an account of an event, a situation, or a person's progress. It explains something to readers that they didn't know before and suggests what might be done next.

Before you write a report, consider:

- who wants the report?
- why do they want it?
- what are they going to do with it?
- what exactly do they want the report to cover?
- what should not be included in the report?
- what should happen as a result of this report?

The format of a report is usually as follows:

- an **outline** of the position
- a description of the **problem**
- an **examination** of the possibilities
- a proposal or **conclusion**.

Reports often give information about a recent happening. Their main focus is to make readers aware of a particular issue.

Read the following report on children helping out at home and answer the questions that follow.

*'Hey, kids, it doesn't have to be a chore.'*
*Most children would baulk at the idea of doing some housework, but it can help them as well as their parents.*

*Raisa is a 15-year-old north London schoolgirl studying for 12 GCSEs. Like her classmates, she knows her French verbs and the rudiments of classical civilisation, but she also possesses skills that many of her contemporaries lack: she can and does clean.*

*Is it a parent's fault that children do not help out?*
*Yes. Many over-thirties were brought up to help out with domestic chores and even found a sense of satisfaction doing them. Yet, in Britain, we now spend some £4 billion a year on domestic help. Nannies and cleaners are the fastest-growing sector of our economy: working mothers spend ninety per cent of their salaries on keeping the household running. Of an average £864 after tax, £808 goes on childcare and domestic help, including £26 a month on someone to do the ironing, £46 on a gardener and £9 on window cleaners.*

*What should parents do?*
*'As a parent you have two jobs,' says Linda Blair, a clinical psychologist. 'You should give self-confidence to your children by saying "I love you". Second, you have to make yourself redundant.' An American newspaper recently published a guide to the kind of tasks children can perform at various ages. At three, they should be able to clear their toys away into a box. At fourteen to seventeen they should be cleaning the shower and toilet and mowing the lawn.*

*Dr Woolfson says you should start children on chores before the age of twelve when parental approval still matters. 'By and large we don't expect children to take part, and that's a shame.'*

## TASKS

1   What is the starting point for this report?
2   What issue is raised in this report?
3   Where does the report use facts and figures to help the reader to understand the issues?
4   How does the report draw the reader's attention to different aspects of the issue?

# Planning a Report

You have been asked by your school principal to write a report on the different study and leisure activities prevalent amongst Leaving Cert students. Write out the text of the report, which is to be published in the next school newsletter. Consider:

- what am I to write about? (Content)
  The different study and leisure activities amongst the student's peers

- to whom am I writing? (Audience)
  The readers of the school newsletter

- why am I writing this? (Purpose)
  To give information and proposals about this issue

- what should the shape be? (Format and layout)
  A report. Many reports use bullet points and have a memo-like format

- what should the tone be? (Register)
  The language should be formal because of the nature of the task.

## *PLAN*

**Report on study and leisure activities of Leaving Cert students**

Section 1:
Introduction. State the aims of the report.

*The aim of this report is to examine ...*

Section 2:
Summarise the study activities of the students, detailing what is satisfactory and what is a problem.

*The number of young people in sixth year studying every night is ...*

Section 3:
Summarise the leisure activities of the students, detailing what is satisfactory and what is a problem.

*Leisure activities account for ...*

Section 4:
Conclude where there is a conflict of interest.

*The figures above lead us to conclude that ...*

Section 5:
Suggest possible remedies.

*Arising from these conclusions we recommend that the following steps are taken as a matter of urgency ...*

## SAMPLE ANSWER

### Aim

*During the month of March, a study was carried out in the school through the use of surveys, group brainstorming sessions and interviews with 120 of the sixth-year students in our school, St Fursey's College, Rathmines. The purpose of the investigation was to gather information on the various homework and study practices of the students. The report was requested by the school principal, Mr D. Murphy, as he had been approached by several parents who were anxious that their sons and daughters were not focusing on their work in school.*

### Study Practices

*Students' attitude to homework was to do the minimum required. Seventy-six per cent admitted to only ever attempting written work, unless there was a test the next day. Forty-three per cent of students stated that they did some or all of their homework during break and lunchtime. Many students complained that they did not know what to study as they did not have a good grasp of the overall content of the course and the shape of the exam paper.*

### Leisure Activities

*Most students (sixty-seven per cent) socialised on average three times a week. Forty-two per cent were working part-time to fund their social lives and their mobile phone bills. Extra-curricular activities such as games and music took two afternoons a week for practice and rehearsal. Seventy-five per cent of students watched at least four soaps per week; this accounted for three hours per night. Students organised their study around their leisure activities rather than organising their leisure activities around their study.*

### Conclusions

*Students' focus seems to be on their leisure activities rather than their school work. There is little emphasis on study and learning, the emphasis is on written work. Students seem concerned with the lack of information on exam technique and organisation of course work.*

### Recommendations

*Arising from these conclusions, and as a matter of urgency, it is suggested that a study seminar, which would cover study techniques and exam format, should be held this term. Teachers should be invited to make a plan of revision for their respective subjects. Parents should be advised to curb students' part-time work in the months prior to the exams, and to encourage good study practices by switching off the TV. Students should be reminded that it is THEIR exam which is taking place in June.*

## TASK

You have been asked by your principal to write a report on underage drinking among the Junior Cert students. The report will be published in the next school newsletter.

# CHAPTER 3
# DIARY WRITING

A diary is a **personal account** of what someone thinks, feels or sees in his or her daily life. The diary writer is usually writing to him/herself or even to the diary itself.

Diary entries are interesting to read because they give a personal view of events, situations and people. They sometimes include judgements and opinions as well as facts. Diaries usually include the date, a description of what happened, and how the writer feels. The language is chatty and informal.

Diaries are used to:

- express inner thoughts and ideas
- record situations or a way of life
- give opinions
- entertain or interest an audience
- record travels.

*Dear Diary, Today I Conquered the Roof of the World!*
*Dr Clare O'Leary gives her amazing account of how she cheated death to become the first Irishwoman to conquer Everest.*

*April 17: Forty degrees below*
*As we started out, I noticed there were only Sherpas on the route – no foreigners – and this worried me too; had we made a wrong decision?*

As we continued upwards, the weather began to clear, the winds stopped and the sun rose. I started to relax and enjoy things more. After five hours, we reached Camp 1. My legs had stopped working; I was tired, thirsty and hungry. I didn't know how I was going to keep climbing for another four hours. Pat passed me some hot juice for energy.

Soon we were on the move again. I hated being the slowest. When we reached Camp 2, I was wrecked and had a bad headache. I went to bed almost immediately although it was only 3 p.m.

### May 5: Utterly exhausted

'Hurry up, Clare, it's 6.45 a.m.' I was jolted out of my sleep. 'What's up?' I asked, wondering for a minute where I was.

'The winds have settled a little and we're going to go for it; we leave in 15 minutes.'

We started to move at 7.10 a.m. We walked for over two hours across the glacier. As I gazed up the steep Lohtse face I could see tiny figures like ants balancing on it. A wave of terror passed over me and I wondered if I was really up for this. I used my jumar exactly as I had learned. If I slipped I knew I would fall a long, long way.

It was a long 6–7 hours before we reached our tent, where I managed to drink a little black tea and then fell asleep – utterly exhausted.

### May 12–13: Assault on the summit

Pat got a weather forecast text message sent to his phone and it looks like the weather high on the mountain is going to be good for climbing in the next few days.

I took my Irish flag out of my suitcase and packed it carefully into the bottom of my rucksack; as I did so, I was thinking of what it would be like when we reached the summit and how proud I'd be to wave the tricolour and claim to be the first Irishwoman to reach the summit of Mount Everest!

### May 18: On top of the world (29,035ft)

I made it! I made it to the summit of Mount Everest! At 6.45 this morning, Pat, Pemba, Lhakpa, Nang Chemmi, Jangbu, Lamababu and I took our final steps onto the top of the world. I've never felt as happy in my whole life!

The view was amazing as the whole world lay under our feet.

After taking loads of pictures and calling Base Camp and our families back home, we started to make our way back down to the South Col, where I am resting at the moment.

I'm so exhausted, all I want to do is sleep!

## TASKS

1   What different elements is this diary recording? (Check the introductory list.)

2   Give two examples of the writer's chatty, informal style.

3   Did you find this diary interesting? Give reasons for your answer.

## SAMPLE ANSWER

A Disastrous Holiday

Write three or four diary entries that record the details of an unhappy foreign holiday (real or imaginary) that you experienced.

### 22 July
*Dear Diary,*

*I've been here a week now but it feels as though I've been here a year. I'm counting down the days until I get home – fourteen to be exact. There are six people in the family with whom my uncle does business. They are polite to me, but make me feel such an inconvenience. I thought that I would be minding children, but all four children are older than me. The father, Pierre, is away a lot and the mother, Marie-Claire, seems to suffer from depression. She drinks alcohol like water and yesterday I was in the car with her and I was afraid that we would crash because she was so intoxicated. Mum rang the house last night, but I heard Marie-Claire saying that I had gone swimming with Sophie, their youngest daughter. She had hung up by the time I reached the telephone. I really want to talk to my Mum and Dad, but I can't complain, they have spent good money on my airfare and I can't come home early. Keep positive – only two weeks left – I'll do it!*

### 1 August
*Dear Diary,*

*I'M GOING HOME IN FOUR DAYS! I really can't wait! I have only talked to Mum once since I came here and that was when I answered the phone myself. I didn't tell her how unhappy I was, I didn't want to worry her. Each day here is so long and I've nothing to do! I sit in the garden all day while Sophie and her two older sisters and brother go the beach and go shopping. I've no transport to any of these places. I am becoming increasingly more paranoid that they are laughing at me. I haven't learnt anything since arriving here as no-one talks to me to help me practise my French. I know I only have four days left but I hope they pass quickly because I really want to go home!*

*5 August*
*Dear Diary,*

*At last I am sitting on the Aer Lingus plane, breathing a huge sigh of relief. Marie-Claire drove at breakneck speed this morning and dumped me and my suitcase at the airport, turned on her heel and went in search of 'refreshments'! That was the last I saw of her. My flight was called and here I am. It is definitely 'Adieu' to France and the family ... and the holiday from hell.*

## EXAMINER'S COMMENT

The candidate showed a clear appreciation of the task of writing three diary entries. The appropriate register was adopted and sustained throughout. The writing was always interesting and lively, with the genuine feel of a real diary. Grade A1.

## ASSIGNMENT

Write three or four diary entries that record a disastrous or amusing event (real or imaginary).

# CHAPTER 4
# LETTER WRITING

*Letter writing is a disappearing pleasure.*
Justine McCarthy

In exams you may be asked to write a letter, fax or e-mail for a particular purpose (e.g. to complain, to persuade, to express an opinion). You may be asked to write for a particular audience. You may be asked to reply to another letter writer or to express your views to a wider audience in a letter to a newspaper.

Some letters are written in an informal style, according to their audience and the purpose. For example, a letter written to a friend would be written in an informal style.

*Nosila Point*

*Fintown*

*Co. Wexford*

*Dear Mam,*

*How are things at home? All well, I hope. I miss everyone so much. Send all of them my love, even Joey the mutt! I've so much to tell you I don't even know where to begin.*

*Love,*

*Clare*

**Note:** shortened words help to create an informal style, as does the use of colloquialisms.

A letter on a more serious topic is usually presented in a more formal style.

*Hillgrove*

*St Mary's Road*

*Limerick*

*Dear Editor*

*This year the Society of St Martin de Porres celebrates 160 years of unbroken service to the poor and vulnerable in Ireland. It is the largest volunteer organisation in the country with a proud tradition of supporting and championing the rights of the poorest members of society.*

*Through the **Leitrim Examiner** I would like to invite all local members of the Society to a special event being held in the RDS in Dublin on 30 May. We hope that most of our members and their families will take the time to attend what will be a marvellous day.*

*Full details are available from the local conference.*

*The Members' Day is an opportunity to pause and give thanks for the past, to celebrate and value the work of today and to imagine and shape the future. The President of Ireland, Mary McAleese, will launch the day, Archbishop Martin will celebrate Mass for us and we will be joined by José Garcia, our International President, together with thirteen African Society Presidents.*

*Every year, thanks to the support of our dedicated volunteers, the St Martin de Porres Society touches the lives of 200,000 people. Every day, we visit families, patients in hospital, and people in prison. We run 600 housing units and eighteen hostels, which together provide 1,200 beds for people in need of housing. We also run 120 'As Good As New' shops around the country, nine holiday homes, twelve day-care and family resource centres, almost forty breakfast clubs and many other services.*

*I would like to thank all your readers for their generous support over the years. I am looking forward to meeting up with old friends and new.*

*Yours most sincerely,*

*Padraig Ó Murchú*

*President of the Society of St Martin de Porres*

## TASK

Find three examples of formal vocabulary and sentence structure in Padraig Ó Murchú's letter.

---

## EXAM TIP

Always make a plan before you tackle letter-writing in the exam.

Keep in mind:

- who will read your letter
- how you will begin your letter
- how many points you will include: four or five is usually sufficient
- the sort of ending you will need for your letter; for example, an informal letter to a friend would end with 'See you soon'; a more formal letter would end with 'Yours sincerely'
- will you begin with your most powerful point or will you end with it?

---

## ASSIGNMENT

**Either:**

Write your own letter to a newspaper expressing your views on the introduction of six shorter terms in the school year instead of three long ones as at present.

(Your purpose is to express your views clearly and sensibly, and to persuade readers to agree with you. Think about the techniques of persuasive writing (see page 23) before you begin.)

**Or:**

Imagine you are a person living in a shanty town on the outskirts of a large city in South America. Write an open letter describing your life and circumstances. Remember:

- you will be expected to present a letter format
- assume the persona of a shanty town-dweller living a subsistence way of life
- reference should be made to this lifestyle – circumstances, social environment, family structure, work etc.
- decide on the appropriate language: formal/informal; serious/frivolous.

You will be rewarded for:

- a clear appreciation of the task
- your sense of lifestyle and circumstances
- consistency of register adopted.

## *SAMPLE PLAN*

*I am in favour of six school terms per year.*

- *improved exam results*
- *school work is tiring*
- *teachers would appreciate this change*
- *summer holidays are too long – boredom results.*

# Persuasive Letters

Letters are often written to persuade the reader to change their opinion about something. Employing persuasive devices in your own writing and manipulating your sentence structure can make your message or argument more powerful.

Most persuasive texts use some or all of the following devices:

- emotive language
- repetition
- rhetorical questions
- presenting opinion as fact.

Letters are often intended to be persuasive. Examples include:

- charity or campaign letters
- letters to newspapers expressing an opinion
- a letter of application for a job.

## SAMPLE LETTERS

Write a short series of letters exchanging opposing points of view about an emotive subject.

*Tia Towtell (Alcohol Awareness Campaigner) versus Ivana Margharita (Drinks Correspondent, the **Wallbanger Journal**)*

*Dear Ivana,*

*Alcohol rots our livers, shortens lives, causes fatal accidents, poisons our children, results in teenage pregnancy, encourages domestic violence and public disorder, leads to criminal activities, places a burden on our health service, and costs our economy untold billions of pounds each year.*

*For this disastrous price we enjoy what? A few hours of foolish behaviour conveniently forgotten the next day – if we're lucky – and the delights of the painful hangover. We should grow up and just say 'No'.*

*Yours,*

*TT*

*Dear TT,*

*Drinking alcohol allows us to unwind. The comfort of alcohol's warm glow in our bellies encourages us to socialise, to laugh, and even to be more passionate.*

*Alcohol dates back at least as far as the written word. Its effects permit us to step into a world of playfulness. We are permitted to be silly, if only for a short time.*

*Yours,*

*IM*

*Dear Ivana,*

*It's all very romantic to talk of laughter and passion as a result of alcohol. But what about being capable of taking vital decisions?*

*What good is passion to a fifteen-year-old girl once she wakes up to find herself with an unwanted pregnancy? Where will the laughter come from when the policeman tells a father that his child has been killed by a drunk driver?*

*Yours,*

*TT*

*Dear TT,*

*Your fifteen-year-old girl is clearly too inexperienced to handle herself with drink. Your drunken driver is a fact of life, not a person who decided to become drunk and put others' lives at risk.*

*Alcohol no more causes these things than God does – it's us humans who raise the glass to our lips.*

*Yours,*

*IM*

*Dear Ivana,*

*If people were responsible, as you claim, how could they avoid knowing that drink driving kills? How could they fail to understand that alcohol is a toxin that places deadly strains on their health?*

*People often drink because they want to escape their responsibilities. They need telling, and telling often, that alcohol is no solution.*

*Yours,*

*TT*

*Dear TT,*

*The vast majority of people DO know that drink driving kills, and that excessive drinking is bad for health. We avoid both.*

*You seem eager to make millions of responsible drinkers feel guilty for their bit of fun, while making no difference to the real problem – the sad minority.*

*Yours,*

*IM*

## TASKS

1   Pick out three examples of the techniques of persuasive writing (such as emotive language, repetition, rhetorical questions, presenting opinion as fact) from the above series of letters.

2   How would you describe the tone of these letters (the voice used)?

3   Has this made the message more palatable to the average reader? Why?

## ASSIGNMENT

**Either:**

Write a persuasive letter expressing your views about cruelty to animals. Use some of the techniques of persuasive writing that were examined here.

**Or:**

Write a short series of letters that set out opposing points of view on an emotive subject. Perhaps you could use the letters above as a model for your answer.

*A letter's voice never fades.*
Justine McCarthy

# CHAPTER 5
# WRITING A SPEECH

Some kinds of speech and writing are deliberately presented from one viewpoint, e.g. debating speeches. Others may have a different function, e.g. welcoming a VIP to your school. In all cases, however, speeches are 'public' exercises – and the sense of a public performance will always be expected.

Speeches often call for argument and instruction as well as persuasion. The important thing to remember is that whatever the speech you are preparing, it needs to be planned.

## Introduction

- address your audience
- keep it short and to the point
- make it clear what the speech is about
- capture the attention of the reader/listener.

## Main Body

- logical argument
- back it up with facts
- answer counter-arguments, using facts and common sense
- use emotion, real-life examples and quotes.

# Summary and Conclusion

Summarise the main arguments and end with a snappy concluding statement or question.

## SAMPLE PLAN

### Introduction
*Save the environment by recycling.*

### Main Body
- *stress the advantages of a clean city, countryside, unpolluted beaches and rivers*
- *show how recycling actually reduces the costs of production*
- *add figures and statistics to show current and projected problems.*

### Conclusion
*'It's up to you.'*

*Win: a pleasant, safe and healthy environment.*

*Lose: an unhygienic, foul and disease-ridden place to live.*

*'What will you choose for you and your children?'*

## TASK

Based on the example above, make out a plan for a speech for **or** against one of the following.

1   The smoking ban in pubs and restaurants does Ireland proud.
2   Dublin is a tourist's dream city.
3   Boxing should have no place in a civilised society.

# Useful Tips

- use **logical reasoning** – if the reasoning is flawed, the speech will fail
- use **definite language** – 'will' instead of 'might', 'all' instead of 'some'
- add **emotion** to your argument – make people sit up and take notice, but be realistic
- use an **analogy** – a memorable image will impress the listener/reader
- refer to **ethical beliefs** (these are commonly held beliefs about right and wrong)

- **avoid complicated statistics,** which might lose the audience
- use opinions from **experts** to give backing to your argument
- use **relevant quotations** and real-life examples
- make your positive points **personal** – 'We all believe ...'
- use **rhetorical questions** – 'Do you think this is acceptable in a civilised society?'
- put yourself **in your audience's shoes** – 'A concern that many of you are sure to have is ...'
- **challenge expectations** – come at the issue from a different point of view.

## SAMPLE SPEECH

*Write a speech for your TD to use to persuade fellow TDs to vote for more money to be made available for foreign aid.*

### Plan

- *begin by appealing to TDs for their support in increasing aid*

- *give examples of how people are suffering around the world*

- *show how foreign aid can make a difference*

- *conclude with an emotional appeal about how they should vote.*

*Fellow TDs of all persuasions, I come before you to appeal for your help in providing aid to the poorest countries in the world. I come before you certain that you will want to help those in this world of ours who are suffering.*

*In Somalia, children are starving. They exist on meagre amounts of rice. No doubt you have seen them on television, with swollen round bellies and legs like sticks. In South Africa, many people are dying from Aids. Mothers and fathers look on helplessly whilst their children waste away with the disease. In Romania, for many years, the old, the disabled and the orphans have been locked away. We have all seen pictures of young children in orphanages who have no toys to play with and instead rock backwards and forwards, their shaved heads making them look as if they are from a concentration camp. In other parts of the world that are torn apart by war, there are children who have lost limbs due to mines exploding on land where they have been playing.*

*Can we look away? Can we allow such suffering to continue? Can we go on with our lives, whilst in another part of our world children are crying to be fed?*

*You may ask, why should we give to those in other parts of the world? By helping set up projects in the Third World, we can give men and women the tools they need to help themselves – to build a future without poverty, illness and lack of education. This is what they ask of us – not handouts, but the chance to make a difference to their own families, communities, countries and ultimately this world that we share. We cannot deny them this chance.*

*Vote to increase foreign aid.*

*Vote to end sickness, hunger and poverty.*

*Vote for a brighter future for every citizen of the world.*

## TASKS

1 Where is emotive language used to add strength to the argument?
2 Identify one rhetorical question and say what you think it contributes to the argument.
3 Repetition is used at the conclusion. How is repetition an effective technique?

## ASSIGNMENT

Write a speech that you will deliver as part of your campaign to be elected to the School Council. It will be delivered to the whole school at Morning Assembly.

## CHAPTER 6
# INTERVIEWS

An interview is held so that the interviewer will learn more about the person or people being interviewed – their lives, work, likes and dislikes. The interview also seeks to fill in the background of the interviewee. The interviewer keeps the questions short and concise (usually a sentence), whereas the interviewee expands (usually a paragraph).

The interviewer adopts a neutral tone, but the interviewee can answer in a chatty, informal way. The interview usually starts with a paragraph outlining the background of the person being interviewed.

Read the following interview with the star of *My Wife and Kids*.

## SAMPLE 1

*It's the hit sitcom that prides itself on tackling the issues affecting young people today, and while **My Wife and Kids** may not have all the answers, it's not afraid to deal with the tricky questions.*

*The show follows the Kyles as they struggle with the dilemmas of family life. Sixteen-year-old Junior has just discovered that his girlfriend is pregnant while his sister Claire has got an ultra-religious boyfriend who is trying to put the brakes on romance. And their little sister Kady is dating a boy genius. Michael, their father, is worried about his lack of hair and lack of cool, while mother Jay is taking college courses to help her get used to life away from the office.*

*Damon Wayans stars as Michael Kyle. He is also the co-creator and executive producer of **My Wife and Kids**.*

### Where do you get the ideas for the stories?

*A lot of them are real-life situations I have dealt with as a parent. I've just become a grand-dad because my teenage son has had a baby and it wasn't planned. It's something I wanted to share with the world because I think that a lot of people hide the fact that there are kids having kids right now. It's not how I wanted it to be, but my grandchild is the most beautiful thing I have ever seen.*

### Don't your kids mind stories from their lives appearing on TV?

*I pride myself on my relationship with my kids. But if they mess up, I put it on camera. I fired my son and then wrote an episode about it. He was a writer in the show and wasn't working.*

### What kind of dad are you?

*I'm old school. My daughter is sixteen now and I've told her that the money bag is closed. If you want money, she can come here and pitch stories or work in wardrobe.*

### What was your family like when you were a kid?

*When you're growing up in New York in a three-bedroom apartment with 12 people, every day's a party. Growing up, it was always a competition for the joke and it still is. We'll sit there and be talking and someone will always top it. It's great conversation.*

*How would you sum up the Kyle family?*
*We're not perfect. We're a family with flaws. Our children aren't the greatest kids in the world. They have problems, but as parents we try to solve them.*

## TASKS (FOR DISCUSSION)

1   Who is Damon Wayans?
2   What have you learned about his background?
3   Was there anything that surprised (or disappointed) you in the interview?
4   What kind of person do you think he is?

## ASSIGNMENT

Write the text of an interview with a sports or television star for your school magazine.

### SAMPLE

*Pat Kenny hosts Ireland's **Late Late Show** and is also a veteran radio host.*

*What are the main differences between school now and when you went?*
*Well, I'm not in school now so it's very hard to say, but I know looking at the way my children look forward to going to school, it's very different. We dreaded it every single day. So I would say lack of fear is the main difference.*

*What do you think of the range of subjects available to children now?*
*I think it's terrific! I did a lot of subjects myself when I did the Junior and Leaving Cert, but we didn't have the variety of subjects that are now available. We were given a more academic rather than a practical education.*

*What do you think of the Transition Year Programme?*
*Fantastic! I would have loved to have had a Transition Year. There's no real hurry to enter the big bad world of work and if you can delay it by a year, I think that's a good option.*

*What do you think of the level of discipline in schools?*
*I think teachers have a problem. I'm not sure what the solution is, you really need the co-operation of parents. If children misbehave in school, you really have to depend on the parents to use sanctions that are meaningful; but within school it's very difficult to see what sanctions there are.*

*Is it true that you used to be a teacher?*

*I was in Bolton Street College of Technology that is now one of the DIT buildings. I taught full-time there for two years and part-time for a further two years.*

*How did you make the transition from teaching to presenting?*

*I saw an ad in the paper one day for part-time radio announcers, so during my summer holidays from the college, I did radio announcing full-time and I liked it and they liked me, so I began working at the college part-time and with RTE full-time.*

*Do you have any plans for the future?*

*Ha! Do I have any plans for the present? I'd like to keep working for the **Late Late Show** but maybe not as hard as I am at present. I'd like to travel – there are still a lot of places I haven't seen, Australia, China etc. So I'll have to make time for that.*

*Have you ever been tempted to leave Ireland and pursue a career overseas?*

*I have been tempted over the years but I actually like living in Ireland and I'd like my kids to grow up here. But I wouldn't rule out a weekly dash or a series recorded over the summer; but at the moment I'm too busy doing what I'm doing.*

## EXAMINER'S COMMENT

This work reads well as an interview. The reader gains an insight into the opinions and thoughts of the star. The register is quite formal and polite in the questions and the interviewee adopts a chatty, less formal style. A solid A1 answer.

## ASSIGNMENT

Write the text of an interview you had with a famous visitor to your school. It is to be published in your school magazine.

# CHAPTER 7
# REVIEWS

When you write a review of something, you are giving your own opinion. This could be completely different from somebody else's opinion on the same topic. As you have already experienced in Junior Cert Functional Writing questions, you might be asked to write a review of a book, a film, a television programme, an exhibition, a play, a concert or a new entertainment venue.

Remember that a review is writing that judges or evaluates. It gives information about the **content** and whether the **quality** is good or bad. Reviewers write reflectively about a product, taking account of the needs of those who might use it.

You can structure your review into the following sections:

- introduction
- description
- evaluation
- recommendation.

Your **introduction** should provide the reader with information about what type of item is being reviewed. Give the title and the names of those involved and where the item can be found.

The **description** gives details that are likely to interest the reader of the review. If it is a play, film or novel, give an outline of the story, but do not give away the ending or any important twists in the plot.

The audience of a review will usually be people who want to know if they would enjoy the book, play, film etc. You should include your own estimation of its strengths and/or its weaknesses. Your judgement is the **evaluation**. If it is a play or film, consider the plot, the main characters, the acting, the setting, any special effects, the music, etc.

The **recommendation** is your personal opinion. Was the CD worth listening to? Was the book worth reading? Suggest the type of viewer/listener/reader/customer who might enjoy it.

You are aiming to write reflectively about a product, taking account of the needs of those who might use it.

Here is a review from *Hot Press* magazine. When you have read it, answer the questions that follow.

**Get Your Kicks**

*'Mission Impossible: Operation Surma'*

*PS2 (Atari)*

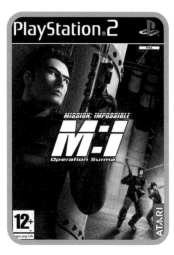

*Your mission, should you choose to accept it, is to take on the role of Ethan Hunt, the ultra-slick all-action hero played by Tom Cruise in the two **Mission Impossible** movies to date, although the superspy on screen looks and sounds nothing like the former Mr Nicole Kidman (his fee was allegedly prohibitive).*

*There's trouble in the Balkan nation of Yugaria, and only Ethan and his elite back-up team can sort it out. High-level government official Mikail Marcou is ready to defect to the west, and he's going to bring evidence with him that links Yugarian President Simon Algo to the theft of highly advanced weapons of mass destruction. Armed with his wits and an ever-growing arsenal of high-tech gadgetry, Ethan Hunt has to infiltrate the Yugarian capital, meet Marcou and get him to safety.*

*I won't give away any more of the plot, but suffice to say there are enough twists, turns, traps and double-crossings for a Robert Ludlum novel, as our hero embarks on a series of assignments that increase in both danger and difficulty all the time.*

*The gameplay is hugely similar to other stealth-based adventures, none more so than 'Tom Clancy's Splinter Cell' as Ethan sneaks around each level, silently taking out both the security cameras and the guards, as well as photographing various people and electronic devices. The controls will take some time to master, as Ethan has an array of moves and modes at his discretion, and that's before you get to grips with his massive collection of secret-agent appliances, from micro binoculars to laser cutters and beyond.*

*Not an original concept then, but a solid plot, good graphics and engaging, if sometimes infuriating, gameplay make for a quality third-person stealth-based adventure. 8/10*

## TASKS

1  What information has the introduction provided the reader with?

2  Why has the reviewer begun with the sentence, 'Your mission, should you choose to accept it ...'? How would this appeal to a prospective customer for this product?

3  How does the reviewer phrase the fact that he is not going to reveal the plot?

4  What are the reviewer's opinions on the game's strengths and weaknesses?

5  Does the reviewer recommend this game?

6  How does the style and tone of the review suggest a particular type of customer?

Below is a typical film review. Read it and see if you agree with this assessment:

'The review fulfils the task of writing reflectively about the film. It uses an appropriate register and gives a sense of readership by taking into account the needs of others who might read it. It exhibits originality and imagination.'

*House of Horrors: **The Haunted Mansion***

*Directed by Rob Minkoff. Starring Eddie Murphy, Terence Stamp.*

*86 mins. Cert PG. Opens February 13.*

*Eddie Murphy's career is widely perceived to have been some kind of upward curve of late – **The Nutty Professor** and **Dr Dolittle** having done the box office biz in some style – and though unlikely to ever come within sniffing distance of an Oscar, his good name still seems to pack out the 'plexes effortlessly enough. His latest opus, **The Haunted Mansion**, though predictably meritless in terms of originality or intellectual acumen, at least has the benefit of compelling awfulness and a consequent curious charm, and though clearly an artistic failure, it may well hold up as one of the more durable DVD cult classics.*

*As strongly hinted by the title, it's a haunted-house movie (strikingly similar in all senses to Jan de Bont's 1999 remake of **The Haunting**) wherein Murphy – preposterously cast as an oily real-estate salesman – and his perfect family arrive in the middle of nowhere (Louisiana, in fact) at the gates of a visibly dodgy mansion, before being introduced to a sinister hunchbacked butler (Terence Stamp in fine pantomime mode) and the house's Master, who sets about seducing Murphy's wife while a series of inevitable exterior catastrophes ensure that they'll have to stay the night. Cue a feast of creaking doors, and assorted jump-out-of-skin spookhouse-flick staples, none of which serves to render Mansion anything other than the least scary film since Peter Jackson's 1996 less-than-spinechiller, **The Frighteners**.*

*Despite its incompetence and the lack of originality, Murphy's characteristic hyperactivity provides just enough life to command a mortified laugh or two, and Stamp's butler is the greatest hoot since Glenn Hoddle covered 'We are the Champions'. Still, we suggest you give it a miss. 2/10*

## TASKS (FOR DISCUSSION)

1  (a)  What is the purpose of the review?

   (b)  Who is likely to read it?

   (c)  Is the language mostly formal or informal?

2  Find each of the following:

   (a)  subject of the review

   (b)  summary of the plot

(c)   positive points

(d)   negative points

(e)   recommendation.

3   (a)   What type of film is it?

   (b)   What does the writer compare it to?

   (c)   Which words are used to describe the acting, the atmosphere, the plot and the ending?

## ASSIGNMENT

Write a short critical review of one of the following:

(a)   a memorable outdoor event

(b)   a film, play or TV programme

(c)   a favourite book.

# CHAPTER 8
# WRITING ARTICLES

You might well be asked to produce a short magazine or newspaper article aimed at interesting and entertaining readers. This kind of functional writing uses a range of techniques to describe people and situations, explore ideas and to convey information clearly. You can often use your own experiences as the basis for writing lively articles that will successfully engage your particular audience.

## SAMPLE ARTICLES

Write a **short, entertaining article** for your school magazine in which you describe what happens between classes when there are no teachers around.

*'And that's questions one, two, three, four, five, six and eight to one hundred for homework tomorrow. Good afternoon.'*

*What can the follow-up to such a traumatising proclamation be? Ms Such-and-Such sweeps from the classroom in a way that lets you know* **she** *doesn't have five hours of homework tonight. The door closes. Almost simultaneously, the wall at the back of the class does that turning inside out James Bond-like manoeuvre you've always seen in films.*

*The fully-stocked mini-bar is resplendent with exotic cocktails and complete with Tom Cruise in* **Cocktail** *mode. Our stiff wooden chairs – probably the cause of more injuries than Mike Tyson – are instantly transformed into leather recliners accessorised with TV remotes for the giant plasma screen that has descended in front of the whiteboard.*

*Everyone gossips about Justin Timberlake's next performance in our classroom (next week apparently) and there are rumours of plummeting points and free college accommodation for all. The fluorescent lights, once the catalyst for mild morning-after-itis to full-blown hangover migraines, are now soft and understated, giving the room a relaxed atmosphere. The lockers have metamorphosed into drink vending machines because we can all do it when we have Lucozade Sport inside us – right?*

*Wrong. As pleasant and enticing as this Utopia seems, the real events of the five minutes between classes are not quite so exotic. Discontented mutterings about failing everything in the Leaving Cert prevail. Stressed cracks appear in the ice-cool students. 'Where's my book? I left it here – I know I did! No – you can't use my bloody stapler!' Mars Bar wrappers and French notes float around the class as countless bodies try to escape a room resembling the set of* **Gladiator.**

*So all you teachers can breathe a sigh of relief, because for a minute there, I bet you were wondering. The staff-room temporarily lost its appeal. But obviously, my wistful vision of what goes on between classes couldn't be true ... Could it?*

## EXAMINER'S COMMENT

This is a lively response that is dramatic and imaginative throughout. The writing has the feel of a school magazine article and is full of interesting details. Vibrant film references and humorous observations add interest. The writer's clever style is always engaging. Readers are shown what happens, and not just told. The piece is very well structured and the ending leaves the reader wondering about what exactly goes on between classes. A well-deserved Grade A.

## EXAM TIP

Remember to plan all functional writing assignments. Make sure you think about the following:

- task
- form/genre
- audience
- persona
- register.

## *SAMPLE ARTICLE*

Write a short magazine article in which you take a stance questioning the role of the media in promoting a negative body image.

*How can the youth of today believe that they should be loved for who they are when the media shows pictures of underweight, flawless models? Nowadays, scrawny skin-and-bones girls represent beauty.*

*Teenagers looking at these images start obsessing about their weight, go on diets and sometimes go too far. Some people dislike their image so much that they have reconstructive surgery to improve their looks, all in an attempt to feel happier in themselves. Others become anorexic or bulimic in trying to lose weight. One of the causes of anorexia and bulimia is social pressure from the media.*

*Anorexics are ideal, they represent perfection. Teenagers fixate on images of supermodels, and try to imitate them. But how can you have the body of a boy and curves as well? In Ireland, 9,000 people aged between fourteen and twenty have eating disorders. The youngest being treated for anorexia is just four years old. What is happening?*

*Image is very important. Nowadays celebrities are pressurised by the media to have the right image and live by it. It seems it's all about being the right size. The image is more important than the talent. Geri Halliwell went from a size 12 to a size 6 after leaving the Spice Girls. Geri claims her new figure is due to healthy eating, yoga and vigorous workout regimes. However, she has made no secret of past battles with bulimia and obsessive exercising. Geri is no longer famous for her musical talent but as someone who changed her body shape. Today that is what makes her marketable.*

*Yet ITV executives have decided that she was a suitable role model for the millions of teenage girls who are dreaming of stardom and who tune into the show **Popstars: The Rivals**. In this job she was awarded an absolutely fantastic salary in effect for being thin. So can you see the message? Thin equals successful. I think not. We must realise that in today's world people come in different shapes and sizes and that doesn't affect who they are. So remember, 'Don't judge a book by its cover.'*

## EXAMINER'S COMMENT

A very good A-Grade response that reads like a magazine article, with the right register maintained throughout. The use of questions involves the readers and varies the writing style. The short sentences in the final paragraph are effective. Simple statistics and examples also add interest.

## TASK

Take the above question on the role of the media and write your own response. (About 300 words.)

## SAMPLE HUMOROUS ARTICLE

Write a humorous article entitled 'How to Survive the Leaving'.

*Shine up your shoes and sharpen your pencils, the beginning of the school year is upon us again.*

*Teens all over the country are returning to their classrooms in droves, refreshed, relaxed and tanned after a wonderful break. (Well, sun-burned and so laid-back you're almost horizontal might be applicable in more cases.) Now it's time to shake off the lazy days of summer and hit the books with renewed vigour and enthusiasm. Stop making faces down the back, I'm serious.*

*I feel compelled to write and reassure you all as you enter the fray. I did my Leaving Cert last June, and the simple fact that I'm sitting here writing this today is proof that it is achievable.*

*I'm the first to admit I was quaking in my boots as I went back to school in August. I had worked hard in fifth year but I'd heard such horror stories about sixth year that I was seriously tempted to run away with the circus and spend my life making a living as the woman who could eat her own weight in chocolate.*

*I won't sugar coat it. It is a TOUGH YEAR. But it's not impossible to pull through it and do well. The trick is to find an escape hatch. Escape into another world by reading a book, or watching your favourite movie. But what really kept me afloat was my friends. This was the major lesson I learnt last year. Future examinees, pay heed! Whatever you do, no matter how bogged down you may be by study, do not isolate your friends under any circumstances. Even if you're too busy to go out, then pick up the phone. Have a moan about the workload or that teacher who needs a personality transplant, and then you can forget about it. I can only hope I was there as much for them in return.*

*A sixth-year class becomes a giant support group. It's no longer everyone for him/herself. All rally around to make sure that everyone pulls through. Honestly, I'm not some mad Oprah Winfrey wannabe. Even teachers become less distant and morph into real people who are working just as hard as their students to help them do the best they can.*

*Don't panic. There is life after the Leaving Cert! Believe me, the actual exams are a doddle compared to all the preparation. Before I finish, let me share a quote that became my motto. In the words of Emmet Fox, 'Do it trembling if you must, but do it!'*

## EXAMINER'S COMMENT

The article has the correct informal register while dispensing invaluable advice to the reader. The relaxed, humorous approach is evident from the very first sentence. The writing is personal and varied throughout. A good A-Grade standard.

## ASSIGNMENT

Write an article (no more than 350 words) on how to survive the Junior Cert **or** Transition Year.

# PRACTICE QUESTIONS: COMPREHENDING B

1   Imagine you are a hotel manager. Write the text of a **talk** you would give to a large group of wedding guests whose meal has been delayed for over two hours.

2   Write an **informative article** for a local newspaper entitled 'Slaves to Fashion?'
When planning your article, it might help to think about:
- modern fashion trends
- what fashions say about individuals
- whether or not fashion really matters.

3   Imagine you are part of a space crew on a six-week scientific mission.
Write three **diary** entries:
- the day of blast-off
- halfway through your mission
- the night before returning to Earth.

4   Write a short **entertaining article** for your school magazine in which you describe what happens between classes when there are no teachers around.

5   Create a tourist **brochure** to promote Ireland's attractions for visitors and holiday-makers.

6   Write a **letter** to the chairperson of your local council arguing for **or** against the proposed building of a big shopping mall two miles outside your town.

# SECTION 2
# COMPOSING

The Composing section is the most important on the paper and is an opportunity for you to show your flair for writing. The list of composition titles will usually be suggested by the Comprehending A texts, which are intended as a resource for students. While you can use these texts for ideas and reference, it is important not to over-rely on them or simply repeat them.

Your essay will be more interesting if you have read extensively during your Leaving Cert course. As a starting point, check out the websites at the end of this book.

Most of the genres or types of language use will be included among the composition titles: information, argument, persuasion, narrative and aesthetic writing. It makes sense to select essay titles that bring out the best in you. So if you are good at writing stories, choose a short story title; if you are successful at debating, pick a persuasive writing topic. In other words, write from your strengths.

# Types of Essay

The most common types of essay that appear on the paper are:

## Newspaper/Magazine Articles

Journalistic or feature articles may:

- be serious
- be light-hearted
- offer advice/information.

## Personal Essays

This might involve:

- a discursive essay – discussing a particular issue or topic
- giving your experiences and opinions on the topic or issue
- giving illustrations/evidence to back up your discussion points and opinions.

## Persuasive Essays

An attempt to convince the reader to agree with your point of view either by logical reasoning and/or an appeal to his/her emotions.

## Speeches/Talks

You need to note the following:

- the audience that must be addressed
- register of spoken language needed
- use of argument/emotional appeal
- rhetorical questions and repetition
- use of anecdote.

## Debates/Arguments

This involves:

- use of points mentioned under Speeches/Talks above
- the rebuttal of opposing points of view
- correct form of address
- format of debate.

## Letters

Think about:

- format of different types of letter
- who is the letter writer?
- who is the reader of the letter?
- what is the purpose of the letter?
- your response to a given problem or circumstance.

## Short Stories

You need to consider:

- plot
- character
- dialogue
- setting
- vivid expression.

# Writing Personal Essays

Composing titles often include personal essays of various kinds, such as newspaper or magazine articles. Essentially, a **personal essay** explores some aspect of the world in an enjoyable or interesting way. Such essays are usually **reflective**, allowing you to describe your own experiences and feelings, or explain your point of view.

You may choose to couch your response wholly or partly as **personal (first person) narratives**. Personal essays also include **discussions** and **discursive writing** in which you explain different sides of an issue of current interest. The important thing is that a **strong sense of the first person** should be present.

Titles vary greatly. These include writing **newspaper or magazine articles** outlining your views on a particular subject, such as relationships, gossip, power, sport, war, childhood, minorities, education, social class, money, culture, racism, media, family life, etc.

Personal essays will include a **variety of language types**: information, argument and, of course, first-person narrative.

Watch the way you construct sentences. If you are starting most sentences with 'I', you need to rephrase to provide a better rhythm and variety to your writing.

## EXAM TIP

**Personal essays** are sometimes called **opinion pieces** or **personal narratives**.

**Q** So what makes a good essay?

**A** Something you feel strongly about and your own personal experiences.

The opening is the 'hook' you use to get your reader's attention.

For example, you might start with:

- a **question** – 'When was the last time you cried?'
- a **single word** – to focus the reader's attention
- a **quotation** – it doesn't even have to be a famous one.

# CHAPTER 9
# PERSONAL ESSAYS

## SAMPLE ESSAYS

'I have lived in important places ...'

**Write a personal essay in which you explore your sense of what a particular place means to you.**

## SAMPLE 1

1 *From the heights of Ben Bulben, you can see Sligo Bay in its full glory. The mountain is a steep climb to the plateau above, but well worth it. At the age of eight, I was escorted to the graveyard in Drumcliff where W. B. Yeats is buried. Since that time, I have often wondered about the strange inscription on his headstone: 'Cast a cold eye on life, on death, Horseman pass by'. Over the years, I have learned that Ireland's greatest poet seems to have been fascinated by Sligo – and so am I.*

2 *My parents loved the area before me and they have been bringing me here on regular occasions. From the start, Sligo captivated my young heart. Some of my own ancestors lived in County Sligo over a hundred years ago. As a young child, I heard dozens of stories about the place. Some were accounts of family life – my great-grandfather had been a hard-working shopkeeper and publican who never took a day off in his working life. Everything was different in his time, and the Sligo people struggled with poverty and sickness. I have been very proud to hear about how he and my great-grandmother helped other families less fortunate than themselves who were in dire need of food and fuel during winter.*

3 *But the stories I enjoyed most were the old myths and legends of the North-West of Ireland. Looking back, I really believed that the place was filled with fairies and leprechauns. I have visited a lot of the magical places Yeats wrote about, including Lough Gill, the beautiful lake he wrote about in his famous poem, 'The Lake Isle of Innisfree'. My aunt still lives near Lough Gill. So do a lot of my cousins in the small village where my dad grew up. Every New Year, we all go back to the old family home for a small reunion (and a very loud party).*

4 *Perhaps this is why Sligo means so much to me. A lot of people associate their happy childhood memories and family life with particular places. Every time I visit Sligo, I feel closer than ever to my own family. It's more than just gossiping and exchanging gifts. There is something special about feeling part of a special family group. Although foreign tourists come to the North-West every year to seek their roots, I myself have never felt like an outsider there. I may not know a lot of local people, but I always feel relaxed and secure enough to stroll about the place as if I have lived there all my life. My dad says it's all in the genes.*

5 *There is a shop in Sligo town where a butcher gave up his trade to make wooden statues. His statues are not simple carvings but powerful images of Celtic pagans. Every piece is hand-made following local craft-making tradition. This man is very friendly with my cousins and he can tell Irish history without any book, and recount tales of old Irish heroes and boastful warriors. As a very young child, I was spellbound by the adventures of King Conchobor and especially the wild exploits of Cuchulainn, the Hound of Ulster. He has also told us about the strong women of Ireland, such as Medb, Derdriu and Aife, often calling them 'holy terrors'.*

6 *Maybe it's my imagination, but Sligo seems to have more than its share of weird superstitions. My aunt is interested in local history and has shown me pictures and drawings of young boys dressed in girls' clothing. Apparently, it was an old County Sligo custom to deceive the little people who were always on the look-out for young boys. Although the modern world would laugh at such behaviour, I have recently read about the traditional high levels of infant death among boys as compared to girls during the nineteenth century.*

7 *She is also very well informed about old Sligo customs to do with funerals and wakes. In the past, windows and doors were left open to let the dead person's spirit leave peacefully. A hole was sometimes made in the thatch roof for the same purpose. Sometimes the bed belonging to the deceased was carried outside to a nearby hill and burned. Strangely enough, Sligo wakes were also times for dancing and celebration. In honour of the dead, there were games, poems, singing, dancing, drinking, courting and even wrestling contests. Needless to say, some of these parties would get out of hand and would sometimes turn into local scandals.*

8 *So, for me, Sligo is a link with the past. I have always had an interest in poems by Yeats – especially 'Innisfree' and 'To a Child Dancing in the Wind'. I like the look of County Sligo and the people who live there. It is not just the Irish past but my past also – and that is important. Most of my best childhood holidays have been spent there, surrounded by my family. To me, the whole county is beautiful and it has never lost its magic. That is why I love this place so much.*

*(850 words)*

GRADE: A2

P = 26/30

C = 25/30

L = 25/30

M = 10/10

Total = 86%

## EXAMINER'S COMMENT

There is a clear sense of personal experience throughout this well-written essay. The opening is engaging and the references to Yeats are echoed later on. Various aspects of Sligo (family, holiday memories, interesting customs and characters) are explored in orderly paragraphs. With the exception of paragraphs 3 and 4, the expression is generally clear and varied, and the essay is very well rounded off.

A little more control with the expression would raise the standard to an A1 grade. Overall, an enjoyable essay that gives the reader a good impression of one county's special attractions.

## TASKS

1   Go through the essay again, making an eight-point plan based on the content of each paragraph. You could begin like this:

   ■ paragraph 1: intro – description of Drumcliff Church
   ■ paragraph 2: family links with Co. Sligo.

2   Make your own plan for the place that means the most to you. Decide on an interesting opening, important memories, unusual characters associated with the place, etc. (If you wish, you may use the plan from Task 1 as a guide, or devise your own plan.)

## SAMPLE 2

1 *For a place to mean something for anyone, that place has got to have memories and in my opinion those memories must have an impact on your life, one way or another. With so many different and mind-blowing places to pick from, it is hard to chose which one is most important to me, which one carries the most memories for me. The answer to that is none of those places do because the memories I have of them are only a week or two days worth of memories and what is that in a lifetime of precious memories? In my opinion, the place which means the most to me is one where tens upon thousands of golden memories are stored with more being added every day. This place, although it is not the biggest or most awesome sight in the world, is the place which means the whole world to me and I get to go there nearly every day, this place could be nowhere else but my living room.*

2 *Like in so many other houses, the living room is the main room, the room where everyday family life happens. It is the place in the mornings where I try to catch that extra few minutes of sleep while I lie spreadeagled on the couch. It is the first place I go when I come home from a long day at school for more or less the same reason and it is the place in the evenings where my family goes to relax. Part of the relaxation comes in the form of the television, which takes pride of place in the corner of the room. Not only does the television provide entertainment and news, it also supplies memories I am sure nearly every family has. I can vividly remember the nervous tension of my mum and me as we sat on the edge of our seats clutching each other's hands for dear life, waiting anxiously for the winner of* **Pop Idol** *to be announced, and the squirming of my dad as he attempted to watch* **ER** *and not forgetting the floods of tears I was in when Peggy died in* **Where The Heart Is**. *These memories and many more are priceless. Although they may seem stupid to some, they do have a meaning and some significance because who hasnt reacted to a television programme in anger or sadness or some other emotion? It could even be said that the television set is like an extra family member but it only lives in the living room.*

3 *This room also plays host to the celebration of the year, christmas. Ever since I was old enough to remember, the living room has been and continues to be the heart and soul of the festive season in my home, as I'm sure it is in many other houses. The intoxicating atmosphere of that joyous time of year is incapsulated in this single room. It is where the christmas tree stands tall decorated from head to toe, where all the cards are put up and most importantly it is where are fireplace is situated. This is the room where Santa Claus came every year and delivered everybodys presents and of course drank the glass of warm milk and took the carrot for Rudolf. One hour later and the room resembled a bomb sight with all the torn wrapping paper thrown everywhere after all the gifts had been exchanged with everyone. Christmas time has*

and remains to be some of the best memories I have from that room and although some of the mystery of **christmas** has been unravelled, the living room still holds that air of magic which can not be found anywhere else.

4 Something else **uneque** to my living room are the memories of people I know and love. Any visitors who come to my house are always hosted in the living room, from family to friends. It is the place where I can catch up on all the gossip and news whether it be good or bad. I have distinct memories of receiving both types of news but for some reason the bad news seems to stick out. I can remember it like it was yesterday. I was nine years old and I was sitting in the chair doing my Maths homework while my brother lay on the floor watching television. My gran **hadnt** been well but nothing could have prepared me for news of her death. The wake followed in the house and even though I did not realise it then, **it is these memories which help the pain**. As I sat in the living room heartbroken, the beautiful and wonderful words about my gran which I was told helped me to grieve and I will never forget them or her. My gran's pictures along with Grandad hangs adoringly on the wall of the living room as do many others to my horror. The room is like a family photograph album with pictures of everybody including the ones you don't want anyone to see, fortunately, I have learned to live with it, that is until someone attempts to admire the photographs.

5 My living room is a reservoir of memories from the happy to sad ones, from the angry to the funny ones, the list is endless and I'm sure I am not the only one **that this is true for**. These memories are what have helped me to become the person I am today and new memories continue to shape me. Whenever I feel lonely or **disappointed**, there is only one place where I long to be and that is where I feel comfortable and safe **and that is** my living room. It is the place I love the most and with good reason and I don't know where I'd be without it. As my interpretation of the old saying goes, home is where the heart is and the living room is the heart of the home.

*(1,000 words)*

## SPELLCHECK!

| | |
|---|---|
| spreadeagled | hasn't |
| encapsulated | Christmas |
| bombsite | unique |
| disappointed | hadn't |

GRADE: C1

P = 21/30

C = 21/30

L = 17/30

M = 7/10

Total = 66%

## EXAMINER'S COMMENT

A strong sense of personal voice throughout the essay and some detailed illustrations (e.g. the family viewing memories). While paragraphs were reasonably well organised and points were developed, much of the content was somewhat predictable. A fresher approach would add life to the writing. Generally, there were too many worn expressions (at the end of the first paragraph, for instance) and some poorly controlled sentences, often running into one another (as at the end of paragraph 4). The spelling and punctuation could also have been much better.

## TASKS

1   Rewrite the opening paragraph with a view to improving the expression, and getting rid of the repetition and awkward phrasing.

2   What makes paragraph 2 interesting? (Consider aspects such as detail, humour, appeal to the reader, etc.)

## SAMPLE ESSAY

'The weekend wouldn't be the same without it.'

**Write a personal essay in which you explore your interest and enjoyment of your favourite sport.**

1   *I have a pool table in my house. I love to play. I eat, sleep and breathe it. As far as I am concerned it's the best sport in the world. I play all the time. During the week I practise for about two hours every day. But it's the weekend I love. That's when I reap the rewards of my hard work. On Fridays I go to the pub. And compete with all the locals. For the number one spot. Saturdays I play in the halls in Dundalk. Sundays I go to Carrick with my cousin and play in tournaments. My greatest ambition? To be number one and prove girls can play as well as boys.*

2 *Friday night came at last. It felt like I had been waiting an eternity. I was nervous and excited. I'd spent the week practising and playing harder than I ever had before. There was a knock on the door. It was Ciara.*

*'Are you ready?' she asked.*

*I grinned.*

*'Yeah, and tonight is the night. I'm going to be number one!'*

*Ciara looked a bit doubtful and said, 'You're very confident. Nobody has knocked Digsby off the top spot in about two years.'*

*'Three actually!'*

*'And you're gonna do that?'*

*I could see she was unsure.*

*'I'll prove it. I'm determined.'*

3 *Half an hour later we were there. I toddled in the door and Ann-Marie, the barmaid, handed me my usual bottle of Bud. I pushed it back. 'Not tonight,' I said grimly. 'I'll just have a Coke and whatever Ciara's having.'*

4 *I waited impatiently for the change and then marched down and put my Euro on the table. Digsby looked over and laughed.*

*'Gonna try beating me again, Niamh?'*

*'I am.'*

*'Good luck to you. I've never lost to a girl – never!'*

*'We'll see what happens.' I forced myself to grin back at him.*

5 *I sat waiting, watching the game in progress intently. Finally, it was my turn. I stepped up. I put my money in the slot. The balls rumbled out. I picked up the triangle and set them out. There was a new boy holding the table.*

*'Two shots carry?' I asked.*

*He nodded in reply and broke. It was a good break but I won. And I won the game after that and so on until I had beaten everyone except Digsby.*

6 *It was his turn. Everyone stopped talking between themselves. They knew this was the big game. The one he would of had to win. They knew if I beat him, I'd be number one. And he would be disgraced – beaten by a girl! He racked the balls.*

*'Break away.' A dangerous glint lit his eyes. It seemed to say, 'Beat me and see what happens.'*

7   *I broke. A good split, but I didn't pot anything. Digsby missed his opening shot,
And I potted the next two and then missed an easy ball to the middle pocket. I sat
down shaking my head. Digsby potted six balls in a row and then the unbelievable
happened. He missed! I had thought it was all over. I cleared up except for one ball
and the black. He potted his last ball and rolled in the white nice and tight behind
the black. I walked round the table checking the angles. I had an idea. But it was
risky. If I missed, I'd lose the game and forfeit the chance to do down Digsby.*

8   *I bent low on the shot concentrating hard. The pub was silent. I played a slow
shot so I'd have position on the black, from the moment I hit it, I knew it was a
sweet shot. It was in perfect line with the pocket. But would it have enough pace?
It stopped on the pocket. I hung my head. Then the pub let out a huge cheer.
The ball had dropped. I blasted the black in no problem. I had done it. Digsby
shook my hand. 'Congrats, you're number one.'*

9   *Can't you see the weekend wouldn't be the same without it?*

   *(680 words)*

GRADE: B1

P = 24/30

C = 24/30

L = 23/30

M = 9/10

Total = 80%

## EXAMINER'S COMMENT

A lively narrative giving a personal perspective on a favourite sport. The essay is
clearly based on experience. The writer's competitive attitude is effectively
established. There is some awkward expression (in paragraph 6, for example).
However, the tension is built up well and good use of dialogue helps the engaging
anecdotal style, which is very suitable for an article in a popular magazine.

## SAMPLE ESSAY

'My family – an interesting group of people.'

**Write an article for a popular magazine based on the above title.**

1   *An accurate description of my family? Think **The Addams Family** meets **The
Beverley Hillbillies** and that begins to narrow it down! Horror of horrors you're
thinking – but it's actually not so bad. In fact, I quite like it because without*

*intentionally meaning it, they are the most entertaining group of people. I know we're certainly a far cry from* **The Waltons**, *but then – as the saying goes – you can't pick your family! Given a choice, I still don't think I'd trade this crowd in. For the comedy aspects alone, they're worth it!*

2  *I'm not always laughing, of course. Especially as I am the unfortunate one who happens to be the eldest, which translates that I am the first to make all the mistakes, the first to break all the rules and inevitably the first to leave home. I foolishly thought that my eighteenth birthday would change everything.*

*'Can I borrow the car?'*

*'No problem – responsible daughter!'*

*'Can I stay over at Jamie's tonight?'*

*'No problem – mature, sensible daughter!'*

3  *Wishful thinking on my part, I admit. Mind you, a change is slowly beginning to take place in the parent-young woman relationship. Both parents seem to be looking at me more closely these days. Perhaps they're thinking about next October when I sail off into the unknown. Perhaps they see all the time that's passed since I was their little girl. It might even be guilt. No, that's going too far – especially for my weird family. Still, I'm beginning to appreciate their concern for me and enjoying it while it lasts.*

4  *Apart from my immediate family – the concerned people – I also have some highly unusual relations who could not possibly exist elsewhere. We all know that everyone has the usual drunken, leery uncle, admit it! In my case, I have such an uncle, but he is married to a very eccentric woman who still believes it's 1968 and everyone's a hippy. There have been so many family gatherings when I wanted to run away from the dippy flower music, the funny cigarettes and the sad dancing in our back garden.*

5  *In fact, family parties bring out the best – and the worst – in all my relations. As a child, I thought it was something very special to say I had an auntie who dressed in flowery kaftans and still wore love-beads round her neck. I felt different, special in a way. She was a larger-than-life figure who sang songs and hugged everyone. This is all right for a six-year-old, but by the time I reached my teens, I was starting to have doubts.*

6  *Just after my fourteenth birthday, my hippy aunt held a summer barbecue which I will never forget. She called it a 'love-in' – and she tried everything to get her neighbours to join in. I had never seen so much alcohol consumed during one sunny afternoon. While my dad killed every Elvis song ever recorded, my aunt flirted shamelessly with every male she could pin down. Two gardai arrived to see if everything was all right. I sat inside and watched her flicking off their peaked caps and trying to get them to dance what she called 'the dance of love'. It wasn't just me who was embarrassed. But there was no stopping my aunt.*

**7** *At one point, she insisted that everyone came inside to watch her home-made video of a 'special person' in her life. It could have been worse, I suppose, but the whole tape was about my granny. Unfortunately, my granny had only been buried a few months previously. So, to keep the hostess happy, we said nothing for a while as we watched memorable moments on the screen. It didn't take long for people to get upset and very soon the whole room was convulsed with crying. Even guests who had never known my grandmother joined in. I didn't know what to do except glare at my aunt. It was like a scene from the old West of Ireland wakes where they used to have professional keeners to chant and howl for a deceased person. I really hated my family at that moment.*

**8** *I suppose I still hate them – my family – at times, especially the children. Most of them are cheeky, spoilt-rotten brats who I have to baby-sit. These nightmare cousins who are little lambs in the presence of their loving mother, but they mutate into fiend-like beasts as soon as she's out of sight. I have tried – believe me – bribes and threats to get them into their beds at night, yet nothing ever works. Only I need the money, I would never go near them.*

**9** *As I get older and find out more about my family, I often wonder if it's the same story elsewhere. Most of my friends seem to have normal, well-behaved families. Mine are just an embarrassment by comparison. My horror movie clan has inherited a special stubbornness that has led to many bitter feuds. I have seen arguments at funerals – often connected to inheritances and disputed wills. It's all very sad and I can only hope that when I am old and wrinkly my sons and daughters won't discuss who gets what in front of me.*

**10** *Having said all that, I still feel close to most members of my family. I even love my ageing hippy aunt despite her cringe-making behaviour. So, what about your family? Write in and let us know what makes them interesting or special to you. Tell us your experiences of family life (post or e-mail to the address below) and we'll feature the best entries in next month's issue, as well as providing weekend hotel holiday breaks for the lucky winners. So get writing! And remember – families are for life, not just for Christmas!*

*(950 words)*

GRADE: A1

P = 28/30

C = 28/30

L = 25/30

M = 10/10

Total = 91%

## EXAMINER'S COMMENT

An engaging and light-hearted approach in keeping with the task. The good-humoured tone is established from the start. Much of the writing is lively and there are interesting pen portraits and some entertaining moments. The controlled style is generally fluent and the effective dialogue in the second paragraph adds variety. The article is also rounded off well. Overall, an accomplished piece of good personal writing.

## TASKS

1   Some of the paragraphs (e.g. the first two) are very well linked. Find two other examples where one paragraph links into the next one. Briefly explain how this is achieved.

2   The expression in paragraph 8 is somewhat awkward. Re-write the paragraph so that it reads more fluently.

## ASSIGNMENT

Write out (in dialogue form) the text of an argument between an adult and a teenager. (About twenty lines.) Possible areas of conflict might include fashion, friends, money, study and staying out late.

# CHAPTER 10
# FEATURE ARTICLES

These are written to present a particular point of view and to entertain the reader. This type of writing is often found in popular magazines and in weekend newspapers. As a rule, such articles tend to use:

- informal language
- humour and exaggeration
- places where the writer talks directly to the reader.

The following magazine article extracts deal with one parent's worries about her child's use of the computer:

*Your real concern now is the amount of time the child spends in front of the computer. Every day in school she is practising for her ECDL exam. In the evening she is researching for an assignment. You are concerned for her eyesight as any good parent would be.*

The extract above speaks to the parent, but the language is not chatty and informal. There is no use of humour and the tone is stilted. Compare this with the next example.

*No, your real concern is the amount of time the children spend in front of the damn machine; they seem to be at it all day in school, and then want to do the same in the evenings and at the weekends at home. It'll ruin their eyesight, make them even more uncommunicative than they already are and generally turn them into fat, spotty youths, fit only to be wrapped in an anorak.*

## TASKS

1  Write out the words or phrases that are humorous or exaggerated.

2  Identify an example of informal language.

3  Where does the writer talk directly to the reader?

Here is the beginning of a feature article about the growing interest in celebrities. Notice the use of several techniques common to feature articles. Note also how the writer encourages us to think about assumptions we make, often without much consideration.

### The Cult of Celebrity

*We are fascinated by their every move, we want to know everything about them.* **Jack Delaney** *asks why we are obsessed with the rich and famous.*

*Some are born famous (like royalty), some achieve fame (like film stars) and some have fame thrust upon them (like crime victims). Sometimes their celebrity is short-lived, sometimes it lasts a lifetime. In some rare cases, for example Diana, Princess of Wales and Marilyn Monroe, it can be transformed into a sort of iconic status. But whatever the causes or circumstances, being a celebrity changes your relationship with the world. From being a private person, you become public property, and everybody wants to claim a bit of you. You are the object of envy as well as admiration, fair game for criticism, interrogation, ridicule and spite.*

### We make 'em, we break 'em

*We treat the famous with a mixture of reverence and brutality. We adore them, praise them, scrutinise them and destroy them. We make them unable to tell where their real selves end and the PR-manufactured images begin. We have no mercy, we show no shame. It is easy to assume that all aspects of a celebrity life are free to be examined because he or she is on show, which means he/she doesn't have the same reality as everyone else. And it is precisely because many modern celebrities are no more special than the rest of us that we feel justified in treating them with such contempt. We build them up and knock them down ...*

### Love it or loathe it?

*So how do you feel when you read a gossip magazine, or tune into confessional TV? Do you love it or loathe it? What can be done to curb our fascination particularly when the glittery sacrificial lambs go so willingly to slaughter?*

## TASK

What is the writer asking us to consider?

## ASSIGNMENT

'In the future everybody will be famous for fifteen minutes.'

**Write a feature article on the modern cult of celebrity for a popular magazine or newspaper.**

### SAMPLE ESSAY

1   *'In the future everybody will be famous for fifteen minutes' – a prophecy from the 1960s that has certainly the ring of truth about it in this media-obsessed time. But who made this prediction? Andy Warhol, the infamous New York pop-artist! Maybe I'm mistaken but with foresight like that he seems more like a modern-day Nostradamus. We live in the era of TV reality shows, such as* **Big Brother, Survivor, Fit Farm, Paradise Hotel.** *Reality TV didn't even exist in Warhol's time and yet he could see this phenomenon. He was fascinated by the public's obsession with celebrity and saw a massive increase in idolatry as people clamoured for more and more information and pictures of modern icons like Elvis and Marilyn Monroe which exploded in the period from the fifties to the sixties.*

2   *Forget alchemists searching for the Elixir of Life, the Fountain of Youth. Modern man (and woman) is attempting to achieve immortality in their own special way ... 'Let's get famous!'*

3   *Celebrity status is the way to go if you want to be remembered forever. Although today's newspapers and magazines end up in our green recycling bins, someone has seen the picture and someone else will recycle the news. The moment Demi Moore was photographed on the red carpet at the Bafta awards with her toy boy, cue acres of coverage in Sunday magazines extolling the right of the mature woman to have fun. Blanket coverage in the tabloids*

of *'Did she or didn't she succumb to the knife?'* And so it goes on, a mad merry-go-round spiralling into the stratosphere. Rebecca Loos (remember the Beckham affair?) epitomises such instant fame. Who knew of her existence before the shock-horror affair? David Beckham was her passport to instant fame and recognition. *'I have been in the newspapers, therefore I am.'* Through her grasping at fame, a family was rocked to its foundations. Like every other get-rich-quick celeb, the question was: would she achieve long-lasting fame or would she be a seven-day wonder?

4   If she is becoming dimmed in the spotlight of fame, will she bow down gracefully, or will she grapple furiously to prolong that fifteen minutes of fame? My prediction is that we will see her on next season's series of **Big Brother** or some other desperate reality TV show for Z-list celebrities.

5   This insatiable demand for fame has led people to abandon not only any semblance of dignity they might have had, but they have also allowed the media total access to their private lives. Why? The power of the media to confer an almost never-ending benediction of fame/immortality. Look in any poster shop. What is one of the most sought-after posters? James Dean, a young Hollywood actor who died nearly fifty years ago at the climax of his career. In our irreligious world, which is so different from the world of Patrick Kavanagh's 'dry bread and sugarless tea', fame is as close as we get to immortality.

6   Today there are so many celebrities that I'm beginning to understand why they are called 'stars'. Not because of their dazzling brilliance (does Jade Goody dazzle?) but because of their sheer numbers! But the cult of celebrity can't be blamed totally on the media. They want to sell their product. It is we who buy it. We are the ones who bought the edition of **Hello** magazine featuring Jade Goody frolicking in the waves of the Mediterranean, an ordinary not-very-talented person plucked from the depths of anonymity and raised to the dizzying heights of celebrity just because she astounded us all with her stupid remarks on a TV reality show.

7   However fame is not a smooth ride. It is more like a roller-coaster. We, the public, are like Jekyll and Hyde, at one moment worshipping at the altar of fame, then descending on these celebrities baying for their blood. We place singers like Whitney Houston on pedestals, calling her a 'diva', whereas in reality she is just a good pop singer, and not a goddess. So when word of her drug addiction came out, the press and her fans went berserk. The mob is a fickle animal.

8   Politicians who have been elected to govern should be the most powerful people in the country, but that is not the case. Stars can convince us to buy certain products, to dress in certain ways, to give up cigarettes, to drive safely, to give to charity, to carry donor cards. I can't really see Mary McAleese or Mary Harney, worthy politicians as they are, convincing us to buy 'shooos',

*like Carrie from **Sex and the City**. On a more serious note, Bono has access through his fame to the world's most powerful movers and shakers and can (and does) use fame for good causes, like the abolition of Third World debt. Bob Geldof helped famine relief in Ethiopia through the use of famous artists to raise money in the Live Aid concerts. They say out of the mouths of babes comes truth. So when all those ten-year-olds who answer the question 'What do you want to be when you grow up?' respond with 'I want to be famous', perhaps they realise something good about the cult of celebrity after all!*

*(870 words)*

GRADE: A2

P = 27/30

C = 26/30

L = 25/30

M = 10/10

Total = 88%

## EXAMINER'S COMMENT

Although slightly disjointed, this piece reads like a magazine article. While questions are raised and some serious points are addressed, the overall approach is personal and light-hearted. Illustrations, examples of scandals and famous names keep the writing lively. The response is sustained throughout, and the register has the right mix of serious discussion with touches of humour.

## ASSIGNMENT

'Television subjects ordinary people to humiliation.'

**Write a feature article for a popular magazine or newspaper that explores the phenomenon of reality TV and game shows.**

You might use some of the techniques from the above examples, so that your essay will read like a real feature article.

# CHAPTER 11
# INFORMING AND ADVISING

The language of information includes telling someone how to do something or how something works, or what it looks like or feels like. It involves describing so that someone can find their way somewhere, or can learn to do something or recognise a feeling. Writing of this kind is based on experiences, research and observation.

When you are writing to inform, your main purpose is to convey to your reader certain information as clearly and effectively as possible. This type of writing:

- uses straightforward, clear language
- contains ideas based on facts
- gets straight to the point
- refers to where more information is available if required
- has a reassuring tone
- repeats key points
- has a clear logical structure.

The language of information is to be found in reports, journalism (newspaper and television), instructions, letters, memos, guidebooks, leaflets, reference books, web pages.

## *IDENTIFYING THE TASK*

'When in Rome ...'

**Write a magazine article aimed at young adult readers in which you give advice to teenagers intending to travel abroad.**

When approaching the composition it is important to identify the task clearly. Underline the key words and ask yourself the following questions.

- What am I writing about?
  Travel advice for holiday or work abroad.
- What shape should it be?
  A magazine article.
- Who am I writing for?
  Young adult readers.
- Who am I as writer?
  A journalist.

- What kind of language should I use?
  The language of information.

- What kind of tone should I use?
  A clear, friendly, reassuring tone.

Now write a short plan.

Paragraph 1 – introduction – the advantages and disadvantages of travel

Paragraph 2 – work, visas

Paragraph 3 – insurance

Paragraph 4 – health advice

Paragraph 5 – accommodation advice

Paragraph 6 – security, money, bags, etc.

Paragraph 7 – staying in touch

Paragraph 8 – conclusion/summary.

## SAMPLE ANSWER

*Alive, Alive O!*
*The Magazine for Young Adventurers*
*Vol 7: Issue 4*

1  *Summer is just around the corner and it is a time when most of us turn our attention to travelling abroad, whether for work or holidays. Travelling is one of the great adventures of life, and should be an enjoyable experience. The only way to make sure is to plan and prepare carefully. Remember the old mantra in your head 'Better safe than sorry.'*

2  *When travelling abroad extra preparation is needed. Make sure you have the appropriate visas and documentation, particularly if you are travelling to the United States, Australia or the Middle East. Your friendly travel agent is invaluable here. So strike up a good relationship with him/her.*

3  *It is better to secure a job prior to travelling. Find out exactly where your accommodation is, the location of the nearest hospital and the Irish Embassy. Remember, in travel as in life, Murphy's Law: 'What can go wrong will go wrong.' If you are planning to go the USA, I strongly recommend the J1 visa scheme from USIT. Call to your nearest USIT office or phone 01 546 789 or visit their web page usit.com.*

4　*Travel insurance is a necessary expense for anyone leaving the country. It is not smart to be stranded in a foreign country, where you maybe don't speak the language, and you are facing a big mess, perhaps a medical problem or theft. Let the insurance company take the slack. If you are planning to take your car abroad, join an accident and rescue service like the AA. It is not a waste of money, you are paying for peace of mind, even if you don't have a motoring problem there.*

5　*Another person you need to check with is your friendly GP. If travelling to an obscure location or a tropical country, you may need to be immunised against such diseases as malaria and cholera. You need more than sunscreen and comfortable shoes when travelling. Bring your own supply of painkillers. Check that the area you are going to is not a high-risk area due to the current outbreak of bird flu. The information line is 1850 342 342.*

6　*After a hard day's travel it is important to have decent accommodation. The youth hostels are of a very high standard in Europe and are worth a visit. But remember if something is wrong, complain, don't just put up with it. With accommodation 'you get what you pay for'. Book your accommodation through a reputable agency or tourist board.*

7　*Be alert, be aware. Some people want what you have! Do not leave luggage unattended at airports or rail stations even for just a few minutes. There is always someone watching for the unwary traveller. Make sure you have secure locks. Do not carry much cash with you. Credit cards and travellers' cheques are a much safer option – and invest in a money belt. If working abroad I strongly advise you to set up a bank account and get an ATM card.*

8　*Finally, keep in touch with family and friends, by email or phone. Even the most remote spots have Internet cafes. This applies especially to backpackers or those travelling alone. It is important to keep your family and friends up to date with your planned destinations. In case of an accident they will be able to account for your movements. Remember: 'It's good to talk'.*

9　*Travelling can be a delight or your worst nightmare. But if you are organised and just take a few simple precautions, you can have a really enjoyable adventure. Bon Voyage!*

*(610 words)*

*EXAMINER'S COMMENT*

This well-planned article strikes the correct register. It is friendly and reassuring while imparting valuable advice to the young adult reader. It is very well organised and the advice is clearly arranged in paragraph form, which is vital in an article giving information. The style is businesslike without being formal. A first-class A grade.

*TASK*

Write an article for a magazine for young adult readers in which you give advice to people intending to spend a four-week student exchange holiday with a European family.

# Feature Articles

Another type of informative writing that appears in papers and magazines is the feature article. Features are articles that are not regarded as 'hot' news. They investigate problems and topics and give the background to news stories. They also include comment, personal opinion and sometimes humour (see also Chapter 10).

You will often see this type of writing in magazine lifestyle pages or colour supplements in Sunday papers.

The target audience wants to be informed, but they also want something light and attractive to read, something humorous, chatty and entertaining.

Here is an extract from a feature article criticising advertisements that depict men as stupid.

### 'Ad Enough?
*In advertising land, women are always right.*

*I'm writing this piece all on my own. I've had no help from my wife, my mother, my sisters or any of my female friends or colleagues. Remarkable, eh? Because if a great many TV commercials are to be believed, I am a man and therefore as stupid as pig dribble.*

*Like me, I'm sure you have lost count of the number of ads in which men are depicted as ignorant half-wits compared with their sassier and more intelligent female counterparts.*

*We see them unable to operate a computer, drive a car, prepare a meal or perform the simplest household chore – the witless husband who cannot assemble a flat-packed piece of furniture. His wife naturally does it with ease, so he has to scuttle off and fetch her some hand-cream.*

*If any other section of society – black people, Jews, or heaven forbid, women – was portrayed in this way it would be regarded, quite rightly, as illegal. And yet the advertising industry is allowed to get away with this disgraceful depiction of 50 per cent of the human race!*

## ASSIGNMENT

'We are eating ourselves to ill health.'

**Write a feature article for your school or local magazine in which you explore your feelings about the issue of food and health.**

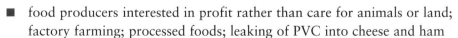

## EXAM TIP

Know exactly what you want to say, then decide how to say it. This is your style. Write to communicate, not to impress.

# Planning Your Answer

**How do I start?** Begin by brainstorming around the statement, 'We are eating ourselves to ill health.'

**What do I want to say?** We are eating ourselves to ill health because we live in a toxic food environment.

**Main points might include:**

- E numbers; food colouring; hydrogenated oil; pesticides; hormones; growth enhancers; slurry; bone meal (a cow is a herbivore but has been fed carnivorous food)
- food producers interested in profit rather than care for animals or land; factory farming; processed foods; leaking of PVC into cheese and ham
- fast food outlets; re-using oil; reheating food
- snacks; crinkle-cut crisps absorb more oil
- health issues
- smoking; drinking; diets; bulimia; anorexia etc.

# Using Paragraphs

Why do I need to use a paragraph?

- to organise your ideas for yourself
- to make it easier for the reader to follow what you are saying
- remember, clarity is the basis of good communication.

**What is a paragraph?** A paragraph is a section of writing. Writers stop after they have covered a point effectively, and at a suitable moment they start a new section.

**How do I show I have started a new paragraph?** Indent the start of a new paragraph by moving in from the  margin.

**How do you make sure you are using paragraphs?** Use your plan. Each new point needs a new paragraph.

# Plan

Paragraph 1: introduction

Paragraph 2: greedy farmers – profit, not love or respect for land or animals

Paragraph 3: interference – pesticides, hormones, growth enhancers

Paragraph 4: consumer wants cheap and convenient food – fast food outlets, pre-packaged foods at supermarkets

Paragraph 5: food is no longer viewed as being needed for survival but as a weapon for an image – anorexia, bulimia

Paragraph 6: other health risks: heart disease, high cholesterol

Paragraph 7: what is being done to counteract this problem? Is it enough?

Paragraph 8: conclusion.

# Writing with Style!

Remember – the task is to write a feature article. There is a need to inform the reader, argue a point of view and persuade the reader to agree with your viewpoint. So the language of information, argument and persuasion will be used. The essay also needs to be chatty and amusing. Look at the 'Ad Enough? example above. The language is informal.

## How do I begin?

Take a strong point and plunge in. Use an anecdote, a joke, image, quote or question. If it is relevant, put it down. You throw a stone into a lake and watch the patterns made by the ripples.

Here is what our student wrote:

*We are eating ourselves to ill-health. Had enough? Enough E numbers, preservatives, hydrogenated oil, emulsifiers, dextrose, flavour enhancers, monosodium glutamate? Are you choking yet?*

*Let me continue: processed, reprocessed, reconstituted, convenience, fast, cheap, toxic food? Never has the world produced so much food – never has it been so bad. What you buy is not what you expect to get. Everything has been changed, or should I say enhanced? No, I would rather state that it has been tampered and interfered with!*

# Checklist on Style

Leaving Cert work is examined using the **PCLM**. L refers to expression and management of language. Is it appropriate to the task? Is it fresh and lively? Think about the following:

- how did the extract above begin?
- what kind of language is used?
- what is the effect of the list?
- is there any evidence of humour?
- what did you think of the last sentence?
- has the student made his position clear about this subject?

## EXAM TIP

A good style must be clear and it must be appropriate. You should refer to the title. Carry the reader along in the flow, as an experienced driver carries a passenger in a car. The reader should see clearly where the vehicle is going. The route must always be clearly visible.

## *TASK*

**Either:**

Take one of the titles from the lists of practice questions (pages 110–12) asking you to write an article and make out a plan, as shown above. Decide on your style and then write the first paragraph.

**Or:**

Take paragraph 5 from the plan on page 66 and continue this in a friendly, chatty style as in the given paragraphs.

Here is an **informative article** on bullying from *Gate*, a student magazine.

Read it and extract the plan or structure on which it was based.

### Bully for you

1 *For evil to flourish, it takes just one good person to look the other way. Turning the blind eye to an injustice, hoping it will solve itself, does the opposite – it lets it live. Any type of injustice is a violation against a person's emotions, intellect, physical and mental state.*

2 *Loosely termed, we call it bullying. Another term for this behaviour is 'soul-destroying'. Its success is due to the fact that it is allowed to breathe subtly. It is fanned by silence, neglect and jealousy. Bullying is a constant stream of abuse, which eats away at those who are being bullied. It causes emotional degradation, feelings of inadequacy, lack of interest in life. it erodes personal confidence, it usually leads to depression, break-down, and in some cases, death.*

3 *The most serious effect of bullying is suicide, with increasing numbers of people affected taking their lives each year. Bullying is now recognised as a serious crime with the perpetrators being brought to court. There are laws protecting those bullied.*

4 *There are different types of bullying. They include verbal, physical, gesture, exclusion, extortion and e-bullying (on the net – through slander etc.). The verbal is usually of a highly personal and sexual nature, directed at family, culture, race or religion. Malicious rumours are a prime example. Bullying through gestures, such as a look, leads to emotional and psychological exhaustion.*

5 *All forms are extremely serious and cannot be ignored. Those bullied are left feeling angry, frightened and powerless, unable to share their feelings with someone else. If you feel you are being bullied you do not have to go it alone. Television celebrities like Patsy Palmer, Tony Robinson and Alan Davies have all been subjected to bullying at school. They got through it with the help of teachers and friends, and through the ISPCC. They encourage anyone who is going through bullying to seek help.*

6 *Once you recognise what is happening to you, and accept that it is real, although you cannot grasp it with both hands, then you are halfway there to solving it. There is help. Do not go it alone. Talk to someone you trust. Do it today. You must take the necessary steps to make your feelings known through the proper complaints procedures. Most schools have anti-bullying policies in operation, so use them and talk to the teachers you can trust. Confide in your parents or a friend.*

7 *Don't forget that bullies are:*

   ■ *insecure and jealous*

   ■ *expert manipulators*

   ■ *obsessed with control and power*

   ■ *usually from an emotionally deprived background.*

*Those bullied are:*

- *industrious workers*
- *good to high achievers*
- *independent of fitting into groups.*

## TASKS

1   Complete this plan of the above article. The first two paragraphs are done for you.
Plan
Paragraph 1: how bullying occurs
Paragraph 2: definition of bullying.

2   Comment on the use of bullet points at the end of the article. Did you think this was a good way of summing up the information for the reader? Can you suggest an alternative ending that might be more effective?

---

### EXAM TIP

Always try to **identify your audience**. Decide whether to use formal or informal language. List the key points (perhaps using bullet points) and put these in order, Decide on the level of detail. Plan how you are going to present your information to make it relevant to your audience. Make sure your information can be easily understood by using clear language, and present the ideas in a straightforward way.

---

## CHAPTER 12
## ARGUMENTATIVE WRITING

## For the Sake of Argument

At Leaving Cert level, it is likely that you will be given a particular topic on which to construct an effective argument. To be convincing, such **discursive** compositions rely on well-organised facts presented in an objective manner. Your aim is to present and develop your views as clearly and effectively as possible.

Argumentative writing depends on clarity and coherence. Take a definite stand on the topic being discussed. What you write should be reasonable. Distinguish fact from fiction and evidence from opinion.

Start by brainstorming your ideas for (and against) the topic. You can then decide which main points you want to make and in what order you want to make them. Support your ideas with **evidence**. When you have developed your argument, you need to draw your essay to a close with an effective **conclusion**.

## EXAM TIP

Steer clear of a sensational or exaggerated approach to the subject. Repetition, jargon, emotive and offensive language will weaken your argument. Clichéd writing is also ineffective. As somebody somewhere once said, **avoid clichés like the plague.**

## SAMPLE ESSAY

'Ireland needs a stricter system of law and order.'

**Write a serious article in which you argue for or against the importance of laws in our society.**

1  *How important are laws to our society? Do people have enough moral conscience to take laws into their own hands without disastrous results? In answer to the first question, I believe laws are very important in today's society but there must be moderation and flexibility. Personally I think that the legal system in Ireland is in need of serious repair. I also believe that while many people may be able to keep themselves on the straight and narrow without any government intervention, there are the proverbial bad apples and they cannot be trusted even when there are laws. These are indeed the lawless!*

2  *I know I'm not alone when I say that I would be afraid to walk home alone after a night out. Why? There are people who will rob, rape and murder. Every night on the news a fresh atrocity is reported, whether it is a sixty-year-old librarian returning home from Mass, or a sixteen-year-old returning home after a party, they never make it. Our older people reminisce about a time when you did not have to lock your back door, never mind install elaborate security alarm systems hooked up to the Garda Station. And the strange irony is, there have never been so many laws. More laws should mean a more ordered society, you would imagine. But how wrong you would be! It seems the more laws we have, the more disregard there is for them. It is as if nobody takes them seriously any more.*

3   *Much of the problem seems to be with young people. A few months ago, we had terrible trouble in our neighbourhood. A group of young people aged from eleven to twenty years old caused mayhem in the alley behind our houses. Drink, drugs, arson took place every night and dare we complain? We were physically abused and threatened. The Gardai were called, but what could they do to a group composed mainly of minors? All the Youth Correctional facilities in the country are full at the moment and judges are afraid to sentence minors because of the strain on the national purse.*

4   *We solved our dilemma by installing gates at the four entrances to the alleyways and even to do this we had to jump through hoops, signing petitions, talking to local councillors, fund raising. Only then could we erect our gates. Note we were not taking refuge in the law, but in the age-old system of a physical barrier. The legal system had let us down.*

5   *But at 4 a.m. the following morning I woke bleary eyed and terrified to hear the squeals of the tyres of a stolen car being rammed into the newly erected gates by some or other youths. The gates were ripped from their pillars. Who by? Thugs! Were the youths punished? No! Why? They were minors. So what can we do? What hope for a law-abiding society when these young hooligans grow into the hardened criminals of tomorrow?*

6   *Then we have laws against smoking with fines for breaking the law. People are left freezing outside as they puff pathetically on their cigarette. If we can have a law and punishment for this, why not for the young hooligan? Which poses the most threat? The joyrider terrorising a neighbourhood, or a smoker?*

7   *It is an interesting comment on our society that a TD could be suspended from his seat for puffing a cigarette in the Dail rooms while those who are causing a fuss in our housing estates are leaving court with suspended sentences and two fingers for the news cameras.*

8   *Then if faced with an intruder and scared witless that you are going to be murdered, like the sixty-year-old farmer recently, you dare not let off your shotgun otherwise you will end up in prison. In fact the intruder can sue you for illegally harming him. There is something wrong with our legal system.*

9   *Our world will never be a crime-free zone, no matter how many laws are introduced. There has to be a will to enforce them and not just on the soft targets, but also on those who consider themselves outside the law – the minors. Of the first four inhabitants of our Earth, one was a murderer, Cain killed his brother Abel. The parents of these two ill-fated brothers – Adam and Eve – were the first man and woman and they were asked only to obey one law. But they broke the one law of Paradise and ate the forbidden fruit. Why? Temptation was more inviting than fear of keeping the law.*

**10** *Fear has to be part of the legal system and that means punishment and accepting the results of your actions. Until this comes about no number of laws will protect the vast majority of decent citizens from the criminal behaviour of the few. If we wish to live in a society we need laws to protect the people, but these laws must be seen to be applied fairly to all, and if that means we have to use some of the national purse to finance the system so that there are correctional facilities available to retrain those who broke the law, in the long term it would be a very wise investment.*

*(880 words)*

GRADE: B1

P = 25/30

C = 25/30

L = 21/30

M = 9/10

Total = 80%

## EXAMINER'S COMMENT

The candidate shaped a coherent and cogent argument, ranging widely in her discussion of law and society. The language is somewhat emotive in places and some of the illustrations (e.g. paragraph 8) could be clearer and paragraph 9 isn't altogether effective. However, the essay maintains a solid discursive approach overall.

## TASK

Rhetorical questions are over-used in paragraph 5. Re-write the paragraph more effectively.

In the following example, the student adopts a historical approach, tracing the evolution of 'the people's game' from its humble beginnings to its powerful place in the modern world today.

When you have read the essay, examine its structure by writing out in point form the plan of the essay. As you read through, underline the topic (main sentence) in each paragraph to help you.

## SAMPLE

'The People's Game'

**Using this title, write a serious magazine article that discusses the growth and popularity of soccer.**

1   *For all its simplicity, football has always been played on a grand scale. It began with whole villages playing each other in matches that lasted days at a time, now it involves the global village, with international competitions and worldwide television. Throughout, soccer has remained the ultimate people's game, capturing hearts and minds from Iceland to New Zealand, from Mexico to Saudi Arabia.*

2   *Though a similar game may have been played in ancient China, football is generally regarded as having started in medieval England. Frequently banned by local councils for its rowdiness and banned by national rulers because it distracted military archers from their practice – nevertheless it survived. Feast and Saints' days were occasions for matches that sprawled over miles of English countryside. Some such matches still survive, although there is less bloodshed today.*

3   *These vast contests were eclipsed by smaller matches played in towns and especially schools. Early nineteenth-century English schools were strong believers in the 'healthy mind in a healthy body' principle as promoted by Rugby's Thomas Arnold. Sport was encouraged and football or versions of the game were widely played. But they played according to different rules. This led to problems when schools wished to play each other, or when ex-pupils formed old boys' teams. So the first officially agreed set of laws was set up in Cambridge in 1848.*

4   *The more formalised game gradually spread until, in 1863, the Football Association was formed, with a revised set of rules. This was primarily an upper-class body. This is seen in the early winners in the first competition, the FA Challenge Cup. The picture changed as the game developed in the industrial English Midlands and North. Factory employers encouraged it as they saw it as a way to encourage their workforce to organise their leisure time. The better clubs began to attract spectators and charge admission. They also began to pay players. Many Scots were attracted south of the border. 'Professionalism' was frowned upon by the FA hierarchy. However, unlike rugby, an accommodation was found. The balance of power moved northwards, accelerated by the formation of the football league in 1888.*

5   *Meanwhile, as the British Empire expanded, English and Scottish sailors, soldiers, railway workers and other émigrés were spreading the game across the world, notably to Europe and South America.*

6   *In 1904 FIFA was formed in France by seven nations – France, Belgium, Holland, Switzerland, Denmark, Sweden and Spain. They wanted to organise the sport on a global scale. But initially the home nations (Ireland, England, Scotland and Wales) refused to join. This was the first example of an insularity that has never disappeared.*

7   *FIFA's first world cup was held in Uruguay, but it was poorly attended. Now the World Cup is the second biggest sporting event after the Olympics. FIFA now rivals the UN in terms of member countries.*

8   *Soccer has become wealthier. In Italy, many of the industry's investors were attracted by the game's mass popularity. Italy's clubs were able to attract some of the world's best players by offering wages far above what they could earn at home.*

9   *But two shadows stain the face of football: corruption and hooliganism. Corruption has always been a problem. In the early days under-paid players rigged matches to win on the fixed-odds betting. Hooliganism has always existed: in the nineteenth century, matches were just an excuse for mass hooliganism. Then came a more sinister development with groups of 'fans' organising premeditated violence.*

10  *What would the early pioneers, the university men who created the rules in 1846, or the establishment men who founded the FA in London seventeen years later, or the businessmen who in 1888 met in a Manchester hotel to start the first league, think of the modern game? But show them a group of youngsters kicking a ball on some open ground and they would recognise it. Africans playing with a rag ball on a dusty plain, us girls playing on a manicured pitch, or a couple of Irish boys using their jackets as goalposts after school, it's all the same game. Today I have tried to explain how we, the lovers of the people's game, all got from there, in the very beginning of football to here, watching the match that I've just seen today.*

*(720 words)*

GRADE: B3

P = 21/30

C = 21/30

L = 21/30

M = 10/10

Total = 73%

## EXAMINER'S COMMENT

This well-researched essay reads fluently and the candidate couched her points in an appropriate register for a serious article. However, the language of information dominated and a more discursive approach would be expected. While the essay was factual and detailed, there was very little discussion about the popularity of soccer. Close reading of the question is essential.

## TASK

'The more formalised game gradually spread until, in 1863, the Football Association was formed, with a revised set of rules.'

This sentence is an example of the appropriate register for this piece of writing. The language is serious and formal, which adds weight to the writing. Pick out another example from the essay that shows the appropriate register and give a reason why you chose it.

# CHAPTER 13
# THE LANGUAGE OF PERSUASION

Persuasion is similar to argument. Both aim to convince someone, to change someone's mind. However, while argument relies on a rational, logical approach, persuasion is more subjective (giving a personal view), and will try to appeal to the readers' emotions as much as their reason. The language of persuasion is usually present in advertising, political speeches and school debates.

Persuasive writing will use a variety of **manipulative techniques**, including:

- suggestion
- exaggeration
- sensationalism
- repetition
- rhetorical questions.

## EXAM TIP

Language use is mainly about communication, so persuasive language will only be successful if it is appropriate for the intended audience or readers. While a powerful political speech will probably confuse (and bore) a class of primary school-children, it is much more likely to interest their parents.

This opening section of a **political speech** (in edited form) was given by Trevor Sargent, the leader of the Green Party, at an annual party conference held in Galway.

1  *It is an honour for me as leader of this party to thank Greens from every county in Ireland, North and South, who are here in Galway this weekend for this Ardfheis. We gather here as members of the fastest growing political movement – people who are thinking globally, and are active locally in every community across the island.*

2  *Our sister parties in Germany, New Zealand, Sweden – to name a few – have demonstrated that our policies work in government – for people and the environment. Only this week we have seen the first Green prime minister elected in Latvia.*

3  *The Green movement represents a set of ideas whose time has come. From globalisation and the inequities of international trade, to the creation of safer child-friendly and sustainable communities, the Green Party is a party of tried and tested solutions.*

4  *The Green movement reaches beyond the tired ideological policies of left and right, and draws deeply from Europe's social movements for peace and justice, equality, solidarity with the developing world, women's rights, and the protection of our environment.*

5  *Above all, we are for a new and intelligent economics – putting people and planet before profit. Green politics is clean politics.*

6  *Green Party candidates must win, and win well in local government elections. We need to return Green MEPs to the European Parliament in June – to address the crucial international issues of social justice, environmental protection and fair trade. The Irish Presidency of the European Union has demonstrated the Government's resolute failure of imagination. Their impoverished vision is limited to the narrow confines of the Lisbon agenda which is all about competitiveness but forgets about community.*

7  *Economic growth at any cost and the survival of the fittest replaces our traditional culture of watching out for each other.*

8  *Green politics is not just clean politics – politics that address the everyday issues of life here in Ireland, for workers, for parents, for women, for children, for the able and the less able. We are alive to the new anxieties that preoccupy parents, mortgage-holders and tenants and those who live with job insecurity.*

9  *We want neighbourhoods designed – from the earliest stage in the planning process – to be safe for children and their parents. That means designing streets for children rather than just for cars. That means playgrounds and parks. At the moment, Ireland has just 200 playgrounds – roughly the number you'd find in one London borough. We also want smaller primary class sizes of 20 rather than 30 – so our young children can learn to read and write with ease.*

10  *We have become the most car-dependent country in the world. Irish cars now drive 15,000 miles each year – more than the United States and twice the German average. More schoolgirls are now driving themselves to school than are cycling to school.*

## TASKS

1  Write down two examples of each of the following: (a) repetition; (b) sound bite (or catch phrase).

2  Where is contrast used as a persuasive device in this speech?

3  What evidence can you find to show that the speaker flatters his audience?

4  'We' is used instead of 'I' throughout the speech. How is this an effective persuasive technique?

The marking scheme refers to **P** (Clarity of Purpose) which really means the purpose of the question, the task the candidate has to perform. This requires close reading of the title so that the question is clearly addressed.

## QUESTION

'We all need someone to look up to.'

**Write a persuasive article aimed at convincing readers about the importance of having heroes.**

# Getting Started

Begin by underlining the key words in the question. In this case, these are **persuasive article**, **importance** and **heroes**.

Then tease out these words by putting in alternative words or phrases:

- **heroes** – people who are admired and respected; people we can look up to

- **importance** – someone who has done something brave or extraordinary.
  The role of the hero in other people's lives. Name some heroes from history, modern life, sport, your own life.

# Organising Your Ideas

You have to convince your reader by appealing to reason and/or emotion. You do this by discussing the central issue – heroes:

- you give your opinion – what you think about heroes

- you give examples/illustrations – refer to people who are heroes and/or events associated with heroes

- you use quotations from the Comprehending texts (on the exam paper) and from other sources, e.g. your set texts or favourite quotes of your own.

Now read the sample essay below (written by a Sixth-Year student). Remember that the essay was intended to reflect persuasive language skills. 'Heroes' could be interpreted very broadly. Some students might write about their favourite hero (or heroes). However, mere biographical sketches which ignore the persuasive element of the task would be penalised.

## SAMPLE ESSAY

1   *The roar from the stand could have deafened a man three thousand miles away, as the ball sailed between the two posts. The sea of blue on Hill Sixteen quietened as the opposition levelled. Mick O'Dwyer, at sixty-seven years of age, shouted at the referee and was sent to sit in the stand. Children watched their heroes play proudly for their county and hoped to be like them. Men and women recalled when they were younger and played for their counties. The players dreamed of holding the Sam Maguire Cup and of drinking champagne from it with their team-mates. Colm O'Rourke and Paidi O'Shea in the commentary box discussed the strengths and weaknesses of each team. Families from all over Ireland had hurried to morning Mass and then travelled up to Dublin for the big game. People spent hundreds of euros on tickets because there's nowhere like Croke Park on a Sunday afternoon.*

2   *In an age where drugs, alcohol, crime and violence seem to have taken over and you cannot walk around towns safely anymore, it is so important that children are involved in sport, music and dancing. It is these activities that will keep them healthy and fit as well as keeping them away from drugs and alcohol. The GAA has been established in Ireland since 1884, and it is one of the most important organisations in our country. It has money, power and if it was a political party, it would be in government! The passion of the supporters and players is unbelievable and within each county, the county players are treated like heroes. Men want to be them, and women want to be with them! But most importantly, young children see them as heroes, and in my view this is wonderful.*

3   *Both boys and girls look up to the Gaelic Football and Hurling players, and aspire to be like them. They dream of playing in Croke Park for their county and of scoring the winning point in extra time! It is very important that people, both young and old, have heroes – people that they look up to and admire, and people that set them on to work harder to achieve their dreams. Every year, countless men and women dream of their county reaching the All-Ireland Final. They attend each match, travelling long distances, and spending large sums of money just to see their heroes play.*

4   *It is important to have good role models and heroes in life. In my opinion, sportsmen and sportswomen, in general, are good role models and encourage others to become healthier and fitter. The GAA is an amateur organisation so*

*the players don't get paid for their hours of training and the endless sacrifices they make to become the best at their position. It is important, in my opinion, to have heroes who are not obsessed with making money, they should play sport for the love of the game.*

5   *Ancient heroes went on adventures and returned home in triumph. Similarly in sport today, if the sportsmen and sportswomen can bring home the cup, they will win respect from their fellow sports colleagues and pride and dignity for themselves. Some counties have never won an All-Ireland, but still have the same energy and passion and hope each year. It is also something special to see a losing side being greeted by thousands of admiring fans. Young children soon learn that heroes don't always have to win. They are still heroic for something equally important – how they played the game.*

6   *The slogan in the advertisement for the Special Olympics – 'Every child can be a hero' – was a wonderful slogan. The meaning and importance of heroes in life is unbelievable and the athletes in the Special Olympics were all heroes when they competed in Dublin back in the summer of 2003. No matter which event or competition they entered, they had trained and trained and trained. They were an inspiration to us all. They were all heroes! Billions of people all over the world watched the Special Olympics and we, in Ireland, were so lucky to have the Games taking place here.*

7   *Though many of our heroes are people who have achieved a world record or won an Olympic medal, a lot of our heroes can be found much closer to home. Parents, children, teachers, colleagues and friends can all leave an impression on us that will never fade. 'No man is an island.' This is true when discussing heroes. Everyone you meet will affect your life in some way or another. My mother, who lost her twin brother at an early age, worked hard at school to get to university in a male-dominated world. She now has a full-time job and supports a family. She works hard at work and at home and she is my hero. I think everyone has someone like that in their life, someone they look up to and aspire to be like. Heaney's hero was his aunt, Mary Heaney. He looked up to her and wrote a poem, 'Sunlight', about her,*

*'And here is love*

*like a tinsmith's scoop*

*sunk past its gleam*

*in the meal-bin.'*

*Heaney realised the value and importance of heroes in life – and so should we.*

*(880 words)*

## TASK (FOR DISCUSSION)

Having read the essay carefully, imagine that you are the examiner. Now ask yourself the key question: has the student fulfilled the task? In other words, has the essay dealt with heroes, their meaning and importance, by:

- discussing the issue?
- giving opinions?
- using examples, illustrations and quotes?

GRADE: A1

P = 28/30

C = 28/30

L = 27/30

M = 10/10

Total = 93%

## EXAMINER'S COMMENT

This short essay really engages with the task and there is a focused exploration of heroism throughout. Points and opinions are relevant and enlivened with interesting illustration and quotation. There is also a sustained attempt to convince the reader about the meaning and importance of heroes. The language is fresh and energetic at all times. Paragraph 1 succeeds in capturing our attention with an atmospheric description of an exciting GAA final. The management of ideas is controlled throughout and the more general conclusion is interesting.

## TASKS FOR DISCUSSION

1   How does the writer create an exciting atmosphere in the opening paragraph?

2   Make out the overall plan on which this essay is based. You could do this in note form by summing up the main point (or central idea) in each paragraph.

Here is another example of a student's essay in response to the same title (on heroes). Read it carefully and ask yourself how it compares to the first sample.

## SAMPLE ESSAY

1    *I remember how scared and alone I felt, in that big smelly hospital room. Looking around wondering what kind of a nutcase people would think I was. Then I saw her smiling down at me as if nothing had changed, when of course it had. It was then I realised who my hero was. She is the woman **that** I call 'Mum'. I never once stopped to think how she'd feel if those pills had worked and done what I had planned them to do. I've heard people say that losing a child is something that **no body** should have to experience. I never thought that I was worth much, but **she always did, but I didn't see it,** perhaps I wasn't letting myself see it.*

2    *Life is nothing unless there is someone you can picture when times are tough, someone that you know will help you no matter what happens or what you do, even if that person has done nothing spectacular in their lifetime apart from making you feel loved and wanted. Isn't that important **enough, but** many people may have heroes for **compleley** different reasons which again is fine, just as long as there is always at least one person that you respect and see as someone who makes a difference, and make the world a better **place, perhaps** it is just a smile on your face but it still matters.*

3    *Without my hero I don't know where I would be right now but I think I have a fair idea that it wouldn't be above land. If my hero hadn't been there for me when I needed someone to just listen and tell me it's going to get better I'd be lost. **Well** I knew it couldn't get any worse so she was right. I have a **tendancy** to run away from problems and just leave things undone if I feel any bit negative about it. I probably wouldn't be sitting here now if it wasn't for my hero encouraging me to just go for it, do my best as that's all I can do and whatever the outcome is, it will not be the end of the world.*

4    *What happens if we all just go out there into the world with no guidance, no one's footsteps to **follow we** might be **okay, but** it would be fairly hard to compete and get on at it if you don't know how high you have to aim. **I'm not saying to imitate someone, just get tips and guidance off an experianced** wise soul who knows what **there** talking **about, that** way the world will be a much better place with much better people. It is not only possible to have a hero who is **experianced** and wise. It could be someone younger than you or someone the same age as you who may have a strong mind and kind heart. Someone that has many hurdles to jump and even though the last one is always a struggle they still manage to make it because they are a fighter with **limited** amounts of determination.*

5    *Having a hero or someone that you look up to can have great power and meaning in **ones** life. It can make life a **much less scarier thing.** Just knowing that there is that one person **whom** can help you through even without words. A simple thought can pull you out of the mess you are in.*

6   *I almost look upon heroes as being **doctors they** can guide you and heal your mind and your soul in a way that you never thought possible by any ordinary person. I'm not just rambling, I'm talking from experience and although I still have rough **times I'm** on the road to recovery and I know I'll make it and I hope that someday someone loves me and respects me as **I do her**.*

7   *Having a hero isn't the most important thing in life, but it sure does help when you feel alone or like nobody **cares, it** makes life seem so much easier and not as cruel as you first thought. Maybe it's not the solution for **every body** but to those **that it will help use the oppertunity to jump the hurdles** and for those that don't feel they know someone that could be their hero or someone they could look up to for advice, then perhaps you will just do your **best** and hopefully do well enough to make yourself some one elses hero.*

8   *To me my hero is someone **that** makes me feel safe. Many people probably have many different **interpetations** of the word. A lot of things which used to affect my life and play with my mind have been reduced and aren't as frequent and I'm sure eventually they will be **completley** destroyed by the love I am given by my 'Mum' and those closest to me. **Somedays** I wake feeling totally numb and **weak like** I just want to jump into a black hole and stay there, but this is something I can now deal with. Maybe it's just part of growing up. I yet have to grow up so I do not know that answer perhaps I never will but I will grow up and hopefully I will get as much praise that I have for 'my Mum, my hero'.*

9   *So if you think about what I've been saying you will see that heroes are important in **ones** life. Maybe not everyone, but some people do see how important they are. I just hope you see that to me my hero is a very special person and if you look **closely you** too will find someone like her. I've been inspired to go for what I want and even if I fail at something I can just pick myself back up and think of the things that other people have to deal with and realise things could be worse, which is the opposite of what I was saying before she helped me through.*

*(1010 words)*

## SPELLCHECK!

*completely*

*tendency*

*experienced*

*opportunity*

*interpretations*

GRADE: C3

P = 20/30

C = 15/30

L = 15/30

M =  7/10

Total = 57%

## EXAMINER'S COMMENT

The answer was reasonably successful in engaging with the set task and attempted to maintain a relevant approach throughout. Points were not well developed and most paragraphs lacked detail or illustration. Instead, similar general points are repeated. The expression was clichéd and lacklustre, including many rambling sentences. There was also a pattern of mechanical and grammatical errors.

# Room for Improvement?

Although it began with a promising personal anecdote, this essay never really 'took off'. Most paragraphs were vague and repetitive. A more focused exploration of heroism (plus additional use of examples) would have added interest and variety.

Paragraph 5 was short and typically unsuccessful in that it added nothing new in terms of development or persuasion. An actual example of a 'simple thought' (mentioned in the final sentence) would have been welcome.

In both the C and L areas, the candidate failed to reach a C Grade standard. The use of language could have been much more controlled throughout. The final sentence in paragraph 7, for example, is far too long and somewhat confused.

Overall, however, there was a sustained attempt to persuade the reader about how support and friendship can be considered heroic.

## TASK

Answer **one** of the following.

1   Although there are several references to one central heroic figure ('Mum'), no actual details are given about how she has helped and inspired the writer. Make up a new paragraph describing one incident where the writer's 'Mum' did something heroic.

2   Using Paragraph 7 above as a rough draft, rewrite it carefully, so that you end up with a fresher, more engaging piece of work.

3   Read the title again and brainstorm ideas to create your own plan for this essay. Aim to write at least six or seven paragraphs. When you have done this, write your own opening paragraph.

## SAMPLE ESSAY

'It happens every day.'

**Write a serious newspaper article in which you argue for or against the need to have a stricter system of law and order.**

1   *Do we really need stricter laws? The answer to that question is arguable. Yes, of course, we need laws to protect us from violence and crime, but not all laws are as **nessecary** as these. Do we really need laws, do we really obey these laws? The news is littered with crime, people breaking the laws. Why do we have laws if nobody obeys them? There is no reasonable explanation for this question but maybe if there were no laws, people may get tired of **commiting** crime because they get away with it.*

2   *If there were no laws, would the world actually be a better place? There would be no punishment for petty crimes, people just wouldn't be bothered **commiting** crime because they get no excitement from it. No chase from the guards, no prison sentence waiting for you, no years of torture in jail. And why? Because they can't be bothered. Once they know it's not illegal, they're not interested.*

3   *Although it sounds ridiculous it may actually be true. Laws for the famous, rich and powerful are totally different to the laws of the working-class society. Take for example Wynona Ryder caught shoplifting $5,000 worth of goods. The minimum sentence in jail 3yrs, the sentence she **recieved** 200hrs community service. Are there special laws for these celebrities? They can afford the best lawyers in the world to help them get away with serious crime. Lawyers, the term means people defending the law. Does it really mean this? The more suitable name would be liars.*

4   *Innocent people are put into prison for crimes not **commited**, while convicted criminals walk free. Michael Jackson, another celebrity, also a possible sexual offender, is able to delay court cases against him. Is it all about money, the status in society, or is it the so-called lawyers? We all want to live in a safe, secure, harmonious **enviroment**. However laws have got to be sensible and fair.*

5   *In working-class society, a convicted sexual offender is given 6yrs, a convicted rapist 8yrs, a celebrity, community service. How can people respond to laws when scandals like this are happening every day? Not to mention the endless speeding and parking tickets they get away with. What sort of an example is*

*this to send out to young children watching their **favorith** celebrities get away with this crime. A law is a law, therefore it should apply to everyone, no matter what the circumstances, whether rich or poor, black or white, everyone is equal.*

6   *It **is'nt** just laws in society, there are laws in schools, **collages**, even work places. The question is, are there too many laws? Has everything got some kind of law attached? Are we living in a world governed by endless laws? Do the punishments for breaking these laws fit he crime? I doubt many people can answer these questions correctly, but what is meant by correct? Who decides on these laws, who makes them final, who decides if they are fair?*

7   *To get away with crime it is simple, you need to be either rich, famous, powerful, or all three. Crime is an act of omission, punished by law. This is the **deffinition** given in the dictionary, but does the crime fit the punishment? The **deffinition** for law is a rule or set of rules instituted by an act of **parliment**, custom or practice in order to punish those who offend the conventions of society. The word 'punish' again. Is the correct punishment given every time? What is the correct punishment? Although the system of law is not always fair or correct, we would more than likely fall apart without it. So there is actually a need for strict laws in society, or is there not?*

*(630 words)*

## SPELLCHECK!

*necessary*
*committing/committed*
*received*
*environment*
*favourite*
*isn't*
*colleges*
*definition*
*parliament*

GRADE: D3

P = 12/30

C = 12/30

L = 11/30

M = 6/10

Total = 41%

## EXAMINER'S COMMENT

This very short essay lacked clarity and control from the start. There was little evidence of knowledge about the subject or any sign of planning. All of this was repeatedly highlighted by sloppy writing, over-reliance on pointless rhetorical questions and the inconclusive ending. Extremely weak in all four PCLM areas, the essay was unconvincing and always struggled to achieve a basic D standard. Essay titles should be carefully chosen to demonstrate strengths.

## TASKS

1   Paragraph 3 makes a reasonable point that the law should apply to everyone equally. Rewrite the paragraph in your own words with the aim of persuading readers to agree with your viewpoint.

2   Make out a list (at least six points) to argue the case for having much stricter laws against crime. You could start like this: 'Drug-related crime is getting out of control'; **or** 'Prison sentences are just not working'.

## EXAM TIP

Remember what you need to do in a successful persuasive essay:

- make a plan (by thinking out arguments, evidence, etc.)
- make it as factual as possible
- make yourself clear
- make it interesting.

## CHAPTER 14
# WRITING SHORT STORIES

'Write a short story suggested by one or more of the images in Text 3' is one of the most popular compositions on the Leaving Cert paper. Yet it is one of the most difficult to get right. Good writing of any sort takes thought and planning. This is very true of short story writing.

The guidelines to examiners state: 'Reward awareness of narrative shape. A tenuous connection with the chosen image/s will suffice.'

J. R. R. Tolkien, who wrote the *Lord of the Rings* books, created a lot of background material for his characters and their world (Middle Earth) long before he wrote his amazing stories. Such background details can make a story believable for a reader. These details establish the world the characters inhabit and where the story takes place.

# Planning Your Short Story

Think of a **plot** – a basic outline of what happens in your story.

It is said that there are only half a dozen basic plots in literature:

- rags to riches (*Cinderella*)
- boy meets girl (*Romeo and Juliet*)
- winning against the odds (*David and Goliath*)
- innocent characters falling into a trap (*The Spider and the Fly*)
- fate catching up with a wrongdoer (*Macbeth*)
- goodness rewarded (*Sleeping Beauty*).

You could try using a chase, a search, a race against time. Or you could decide on a theme: love, money, power, revenge, survival, justice, betrayal, racism etc. But always write about something you are interested in or something that has happened to you. You must be really involved in what you are writing about and who you are writing for. After all, if **you** find the story boring, so will the reader.

> ## EXAM TIP
>
> Narrative writing needs developed characters and settings. Who is it about? Where is it happening? A good story also needs a logical structure.

# Structuring a Plot

## Beginning

Introduce your characters and their world. What do they want to achieve? What obstacles stand in their way?

(Remember: there is no story without conflict of some sort.)

## Build-up

What's going to happen? How will you build up to the climax? (Give your characters a challenge; there has to be an element of risk to keep the story exciting.)

### Climax

Bring the action to a head. The main event or turning-point happens here. The central character will have to make a decision.

### Ending

The conclusion needs to make a point. Give your story a moral. The main character has learnt a lesson about life. Or give the story an unexpected twist. Remember to leave your reader satisfied so that he/she doesn't feel cheated at the end of the story. (The juvenile 'It was all dream' is not a valid conclusion.)

## TASKS

1   Choose a story or film that you know and like. Write out its plot structure by breaking it up into the sections above: Beginning, Build-up, Climax and Ending. Were you satisfied or did you feel cheated by the ending?

2   Make out a plot structure for a story you would like to write. Use the guidelines above to structure it.

# Creating Characters

If you are to create believable characters, you need to know them well before you start writing. You can practise this before the exam and, if you wish, you can use that character or elements of him/her in your exam story. Create a fact-file for your character.

*Name: Josh Turner*

*Age: 16*

*Occupation: student at local community college, on the point of expulsion.*

*Appearance: short spiked black hair, sallow complexion; blue eyes, hard stare; rearranges school uniform – school jumper, no tie, black leather jacket, steel-tipped boots.*

*Personality: looks like a typical troublemaker; teachers regard him as a threat; good sense of humour; loyal friend; doesn't think he's as good as his younger brother.*

*Hobbies: everything to do with pool; listening to very loud music; hanging out with friends.*

*Ambition: to win the region's pool league.*

*Hates: PE and especially the soccer coach Mr Stanley.*

## TASK

Write a character fact-file for the main character in your story. Use the model above to guide you. Add extra sections, such as Fears, Likes, Family, etc.

> **EXAM TIP**
>
> A character is portrayed directly and indirectly through:
>
> - description
> - dialogue
> - action.

The test of a well-drawn character is that the reader should want to know more about him/her. What motivates/drives the character will direct the plot. Depicting this motivation will engage the reader and make the plot engrossing.

# Description

*The legs were tucked into new white football socks, neatly folded at his ankles. Mr Percy's football boots were polished as black and shiny as the bombs used by assassins in comic strips.*

From **A Kestrel for a Knave** *by Barry Hines*

This short description paints Mr Percy as a silly character. But it also links him to danger.

## TASKS

1   Write two sentences describing your character from your fact file using a simile/metaphor to describe him/her.
2   Read the following description and write a short paragraph about the type of person you think Dad is.

*I was fairly organised and excited about Dad's present. He'd love the telescope. Now he'd have an excuse to stay in the garden both day and night, escaping all the women. Three daughters, two living at home and me, just a stone's throw away. No sons, poor man. He was like a gnome in winter, pottering about the flowerbeds in his little woolly hat and scarf.*

# Dialogue

*'WHAT THE HELL IS THIS?'*

*A flimsy white piece of paper was dangled before his eyes.*

*'Well?' his father demanded, eyes bulging, face red – in fact, getting redder by the second, Joey thought.*

*'They're me Mock Leaving Cert results, Da.'*

*'CHRIST, JOE!' his father thundered, making him jump. 'I know what they are – I just want to know, are they for real?'*

*Mr Boland glared at his son and then surveyed the offending piece of paper.*

*'It says here that you have failed everything – Es, Fs, NGs, the lot – now surely that can't be right?'*

*His voice was dangerously low.*

*Joey bit his lip, his green eyes glared insolently at his father.*

*'It's right all right,' was all he could say.*

*From **Livewire** by Martina Murphy*

When reading this piece of dialogue, the reader gets a clear picture of an apoplectic father and his defiant son. The cause of tension between them is also evident.

Dialogue brings characters to life, reveals new information about the character speaking or the character spoken about, adds variety to the story.

Place what is actually said **inside speech marks**. Put a comma, exclamation mark or question mark at the end of what is said.

Use a different line for each person who speaks. If there are only two characters speaking, once you have established who is speaking, you do not have to identify the speaker on every line.

Think about how somebody says something. Use a **variety of verbs** to replace the word 'said'. Here are some examples:

*replied, squeaked, snorted, snapped, stammered, giggled, asked, exclaimed, laughed, gasped, answered, whispered, shrieked, screamed.*

## TASKS

**1**   What does the following dialogue tell you about the narrator and Pete?

*Pete popped his head over the partition. He waved his presentation document in front of me fanning my thoughts away and asked if I would have a look over it before tomorrow's meeting. We had worked on a number of projects together over the last six months.*

*'I value your opinion, you know, you've always got a good angle on these issues.'*

*'Is that the best flattery you can offer me this afternoon?' I don't check out a guy's presentation for less than an outrageous compliment,' I smirked.*

*I was flirting almost subconsciously, apparently this was one of my traits. Sometimes it was just easier to make a laugh of things. Then Pete took my hand.*

*'Would it please you to know that I consider you to be the most beautiful woman that I have ever had the good fortune to meet?'*

*For a second he stopped smiling and didn't blink. I laughed then, sort of quivered, suddenly uncomfortable.*

*From **Shadows** by Gwen Devins*

2  Write a short passage about **your** character, possibly from a build-up scene which shows tension between him/herself and another. Use action and dialogue to give clues and implied character information to your reader. Use the examples above to guide you.

# Get Inside Your Character's Head!

The thoughts and feelings of your characters will be of interest to the reader. What are they thinking about?

What motivates them? (Makes them do what they do.)

How do they feel about the things that happen to them?

Use an **interior monologue** to show this. This means writing down the character's thoughts, as if the character were speaking aloud. The reader feels closer to the character, as if he/she can understand the character's feelings.

*I still could not envision the depths of darkness in which his mind must have drowned. Perhaps it was the lack of understanding that made it so hard to overthrow the guilt. I sought out the signs I failed to recognise. I begged answers he could no longer give.*

*From **Shadows** by Gwen Devins*

In the above extract, the character is struggling to understand the action of another character, and is full of reproach because signals were not picked up.

## TASK

Write a short interior monologue for **your** character at the climax of your story as he/she struggles to make a decision about what to do next.

# Action

A character can also be shown through action.

*She gave no thanks for the help and scowled at the youngsters who had returned her cat. She cuddled the cat, speaking softly to it.*

The reader picks up the signals given by the writer.

She 'scowls' at the youngsters. This is a negative signal. She 'cuddles' and 'speaks softly' to the cat. This suggests kindness towards the animal.

So the writer has shown us two sides to this character by describing her actions. Dickens uses the same techniques in his novel *Great Expectations* when describing a character cutting bread.

*She jammed the loaf hard and fast against her bib ... then sawed a very thick round off the loaf ... hewed it into two halves, of which Joe got one and I got the other.*

This describes a strong, almost violent woman filled with fierce energy.

## TASK

Look back at your character fact-file. What kind of person is your character: tough, cheeky, happy, weak or strong? Write two or three sentences describing what your character is doing in such a way that we know what the character is like. Look at the sample below before you begin.

## SAMPLE

Here is a character who is finding it hard to concentrate because of inner trauma.

*I scanned a magazine for the TV listings. No great films on tonight, a couple of mediocre ones. I flicked through the stations as if my thumb, resting on the remote control, had a nervous twitch. I glanced round the room with its pale yellow walls. I shook my head at the poor-quality plaster in the bay window ... Maybe I'd do some housework instead.*

## SAMPLE SHORT STORY

### *I've everything to live for?*

1   *I sat in the corner of that cold, dreary classroom. The bell had long gone. The sea of blue uniforms had ebbed away. I preferred it that way. The dark green walls were covered in posters and notices. An environmentally friendly poster hung lopsided. Books and copies lay scattered on the floor. Across the room hung a map of the world. I looked at it and wished I was anywhere but here. A statue of Our Lady stood proudly above the blackboard. I wanted to ask her why. Why did it have to be me? I looked at her hopefully, but got no reply. I sat swinging on my chair.*

2   *A faint footstep echoed on the marble stair. The inner fire door swung with a bang. I started to shake. I clasped my fist tighter. It was clammy. They were coming. I stood and felt I could not breathe. I could hear them jeering. My accent really started it. My family had moved to Dublin from the Midlands the*

summer holiday before I began First Year. My Dad had always wanted to be a top doctor, but had to settle for an office job. Money had been tight when he was growing up. He used to say 'I'll make sure you have everything to live for, not like me stuck in a dead-end job.' But it isn't working. A lot of the other kids knew each other from primary school or were neighbours. I was an outsider. The 'thicko' from the country. And I had made a big mistake.

3    It began with little things – throwing my bag over the wall, taking my track suit and wetting it under the tap before gym, pinching me in class. When I yelled the first time it happened, I got into trouble – not them. Why didn't I tell someone? There was nobody to tell. I didn't know the other kids, they weren't on my side, and while they didn't join in, they didn't try to stop it either.

4    The main guy was Tosser Malone. Every morning I ran the gauntlet of Tosser and his mates. 'Well, here's our little country cousin. How's it going? Got all your lovely pens? Ready to impress Mr Reilly are we?' They were never going to let it go.

5    Foolishly, I had really gone to town on the first assignment for CSPE. I researched it in the library and had spent a lot of time on the presentation. It had looked good, but how I wished it hadn't.

6    'A great effort from our new pupil, Jack, who has just joined us from the country! He could teach you a thing or two, Malone,' announced Mr. Reilly, our CSPE teacher. The class laughed. From that moment my fate was sealed. Malone was the class bully, tough, streetwise, used to throwing his weight around. He worked in his Dad's chip shop each night till late and always had money. His group followed him because they were afraid on account of if they weren't on his side, he'd pick on them too.

7    They were coming closer at a run now. I paced up and down the empty classroom not wanting to face them again. My bottom lip began to quiver. Christ! I couldn't let them see me cry. I stared at the map. I had the exam papers. Dad now worked in the office of our school and I had found his keys. Maybe they would just take them and let me go. Not a beating this time. They were very careful never to beat me where it would be seen, just stomach kicks, nothing visible.

8    The door opened. I turned with a stupid grin on my face. There were three of them. Tosser's black eyes bored a hole in my brain. He never spoke. His henchmen did that service.

'Well, country cousin, have you something for us?'

'Yeah, I did as you asked. Here are the exam papers for the tests.'

I held out the folder. They were grabbed and stuffed quickly in a bag. I began *to think I could go now. But Tosser spoke.*

*'Just another little job, country cousin. I want the keys to the main office.'*

*'I haven't got them,' I answered, trembling.*

*'Yeah, tell us another,' Toss sneered.*

*'Right little cry baby, aren't ya? You get them if you know what's good for you.'*

9  *Thwack! A swift thump to my stomach followed. I crumpled to the ground. The boots started then. I curled around trying to protect myself. Then they were gone. Through a blur I stared up at the map. There had to be a way out. Then I heard footsteps approaching again. Please God, don't let them come back!*

10  *'Who's in there? Ah, son, it's you. I hope you are studying for the end of term tests. Remember it's all up to you. You have everything to live for, you know. That's why your Mum and I made the sacrifices, selling the house and land. We're counting on you to pull yourself up.' Dad wheeled around and was gone. Jesus, five more years of this. Tosser, Dad, points, pressure ...*

11  *'This is the six o'clock news. A young thirteen year-old boy was today found hanging from the stairs in his home in South Dublin. Research shows that bullying peaks in First and Second Year among thirteen- and fourteen-year-olds. A poignant diary was found beside the boy.*

*Monday: my money was taken.*

*Tuesday: names called and jeering.*

*Wednesday: my uniform torn.*

*Thursday: I am bleeding.*

*Friday: it's ended.'*

*(940 words)*

GRADE: B1

P = 25/30

C = 24/30

L = 24/30

M =  9/10

Total = 82%

## EXAMINER'S COMMENT

Overall, there is a clear awareness of narrative shape which deserved to be well rewarded. The opening atmosphere was effectively established – as were the background details to the conflict. Characters and dialogue also added credibility. While the writing was somewhat awkward in places, the growing tension was evident and the ending was convincingly handled.

## TASKS

1   Write a short set of notes commenting on the way atmosphere is created in the opening paragraph of the story.

2   Paragraphs 4 and 5 are both quite short. Rewrite one of them, adding some extra description and interest.

3   Write an alternative final paragraph which ends the story in a completely different way.

# Short Story Settings

The setting of your story is where and when the action takes place. It must be realistic, just as your characters have to be believable. You have to draw your reader into the world of your story with careful descriptive writing which enables the reader to picture the scene. This is where you also set the mood of your story.

Use a real place as your setting. You can describe a location you know well and set fictitious characters and events in it.

Read the following descriptions and answer the questions.

(a)   *Heavy blue/black bruised clouds hung in the sky. Squalls of rain flung themselves at the cliff. The wind moaned. Enclosed in the shelter of my car, I shut my eyes and the memories flooded back.*

(b)   *The wild squeals of children filled the air as they tipped their toes gingerly into the icy blue waves dancing on the gleaming white sand. The hurdy-gurdy sound of the ice cream van droned and the sun baked the rows of glistening brown bodies. I leaned back, lazily, and took a deep breath as I stared through the tracery of green grasses into an ever-deepening blue sky.*

## TASKS

1   What type of mood is set in each of these descriptions? Pick out two phrases from each that show you the mood.

2   What type of world is described in this next extract?

*There was nobody expected this evening, there rarely was. When I lost him, friends were great at first. They rallied round and offered support. I didn't really notice or appreciate it at the time. My little world became a fuzz of ringing phones and hollow hugs. Several weeks after the funeral was over, most people felt a reason to smile again. The muscles in my face were numb.*

3   Write your own descriptive paragraph. Think of a place you know well that might provide a background for your story. Write a paragraph of description, including the names of real buildings, shops and streets. Try to create a mood – perhaps warm and comforting or eerie and sinister. Before you start, read this extract from Charles Dickens' *Great Expectations*. This is how a master writer draws you into the world of the story, introduces his main character and sets the mood.

*Ours was the marsh country, down by the river, within, as the river wound, twenty miles of the sea. My first most vivid and broad impression of the identity of things, seems to me to have been gained on a memorable raw afternoon towards evening. At such a time I found out for certain, that this bleak place overgrown with nettles was the churchyard; and that Philip Pirrip late of this parish, and also Georgiana, wife of the above, were dead and buried ... And that the dark flat wilderness beyond the churchyard, intersected with dykes and mounds and gates, with scattered cattle feeding on it, was the marshes; and that the distant savage lair from which the wind was rushing was the sea; and that the small bundle of shivers growing afraid of it all and beginning to cry, was Pip.*

> ## EXAM TIP
>
> When writing description, use the **senses**:
>
> - **sight** – how things looked
>   'Mounds of blue shoulders hunched over desks writing furiously.'
> - **sound** – how things sounded
>   'A faint dripping sound echoed through the empty washrooms.'
> - **smell** – how things smelled
>   'The door opened and his nostrils were filled with the rank, greasy smell of overcooked chips.'
> - **taste** – how things tasted
>   'Her tears flowed and tasted salty as she tried to flick them away with her tongue.'
> - **touch** – how things felt
>   'She felt a crunch beneath her foot on the dark undergrowth, and something moist filled her shoe.'

# The Opening

The opening introduces the characters and setting, and begins to develop the main plot strands. You must have an interesting opening as you need to capture the attention of your reader. Decide whether you want your story to be comfortable or uneasy.

What is the weather, the time of day, the mood? Here are examples of openings that will intrigue the reader and make him/her want to read on.

*I snuggled happily under the warm duvet. Leaving Cert done, parents on holiday, the house to myself, life was good. A faint creak sounded from the hall downstairs. Just the wind, I thought as I turned over. But there it was again, a pattern of creaks coming nearer, moving up the stairs ...*

The reader wants to know what or who is there; what is going to happen next? Will there be a robbery or murder?

Here is the opening from *Murder on the Orient Express*, a famous detective novel by Agatha Christie.

*It was five o'clock on a winter's morning in Syria. Alongside the platform at Aleppo stood the train grandly designated in railway guides as the Taurus Express. It consisted of a kitchen and dining-car, a sleeping car and two local coaches.*

*By the step leading up into the sleeping car stood a young French lieutenant, resplendent in uniform, conversing with a small lean man, muffled up to the ears, of whom nothing was visible but a pink-tipped nose and the two points of an upward curled moustache.*

As you can see, the readers are not given too much information. Keep the readers guessing so that they will want to read on. Never start 'telling a story'. Begin with an interesting description of a character or setting, or a piece of dialogue or an unusual fact or opinion.

## TASK

Read the following opening and give two reasons why you think it is effective.

*Shadows slinked up behind me and purred. He could still startle me even when I knew he was in the room. I stroked his back and he arched and pointed his tail straight in the air. Dinnertime. I reluctantly opened the tin of cat food. There are some smells I just couldn't get used to and the stink of cat food was one of them, uugh. I filled the bowl and left him to his delights. There was nobody expected this evening. There rarely was.*

Here is an opening using direct speech.

*'Why would you go out with someone like him? He's no good. Can't you see that? Haven't we done everything for you? What more could you ...'*

*Her voice droned on in the background. He was my first serious boyfriend. I loved him. Why shouldn't I see him?*

This opening involves the reader because it:

- conveys the parent's edginess through her repeated questions
- suggests the daughter's lack of patience as she lets her mind wander away from what her mother is saying
- sets up a source of tension in the story to come.

## TASK

Write the opening to your story and use dialogue between the two characters to show the potential conflict and so entice your reader into wanting to read on.

# The Ending

In the final section of your writing, you must begin to tie up the loose ends. You have three main choices for your ending:

- a cliffhanger
- a twist in the tale
- a resolution.

## Cliffhanger

This leaves the story without a definite conclusion or resolution. But the reader needs to be left with some clues as to what will happen next. Don't leave the ending unfinished as if you ran out of time. Plan that your story will end unresolved. You should have some idea of what will happen next, even though you are only giving clues to your reader to guess the ending.

*I felt guilty. I knew it had taken a lot of guts for Pete to ask me out. He'd phoned before but never with any intention, or at least never voicing any. We'd usually discuss work and sometimes digress a little on an amusing topic. The phone calls were never long but pleasant. I felt guilty crushing someone so close to Christmas. He didn't deserve to feel bad. I wanted it explained that I couldn't go out with him because of everything that was good about him but I wasn't prepared to bring the words to the surface. My handbag was cast on the opposite end of the couch. It was open and several edges of shopping receipts stuck out. I pulled the bag over ... My address book was buried under the pile. I fiddled with it opening it under L for Lavelle, Pete's surname. I walked out to the hall and sat on the bottom stair pulling the phone over to my feet. I picked up the receiver; the dial tone echoed and seemed to grow louder. I subconsciously tapped the receiver against my chin. I hung up, A little reluctant this time. Not yet but maybe, maybe I was getting there.*

From **Shadows** by Gwen Devins

## Twist in the Tale

This is a completely unexpected turn of events. Again, you should have decided that you are going to end this way when you are planning your story. You can then drop a hint earlier in the plot to which you can refer back later.

*'You don't seem to be a success as a story teller,' said the bachelor.*

*It's a very difficult thing to tell stories that children can both understand and appreciate,' said the aunt.*

*'I don't agree with you.'*

*'Perhaps you would like to tell them a story.'*

*'Once upon a time there was a little girl called Bertha who was extraordinarily good ... horribly good ... she won several medals for goodness ... She went to the Prince's park where there were no flowers because all the little pigs had eaten them.*

*The wolf was just moving away when he heard the sound of the medals clinking and stopped to listen; they clinked again in a bush quite near him. He dashed into the bush, his pale eyes gleaming with ferocity and triumph and dragged Bertha out and devoured her to the last morsel. All that was left of her were her shoes, bits of clothing, and the three medals for goodness.'*

*'Were any of the little pigs killed?' asked one of the children.*

*'No, they all escaped.'*

*'The story began badly,' said the smaller of the small girls, 'but it had a beautiful ending.'*

*'It is the most beautiful story that I ever heard,' said the bigger of the small girls, with immense decision.*

*'It is the only beautiful story I have ever heard,' said Cyril.*

*'A most improper story to tell young children! You have undermined the effect of years of careful teaching.'*

*'At any rate I kept them quiet for ten minutes which was more than you could do,' said the bachelor.*

*'Unhappy woman,' he observed to himself as he walked down the platform; 'for the next six months or so those children will assail her in public with demands for an improper story.'*

*From* **The Story-Teller** *by Saki*

## Resolution

All the loose ends are tied up and the ending is complete and definite. Often this would be a happy ending.

*'O father,' said Eppie, 'what a pretty home ours is! I think nobody could be happier than we are.'*

*From* **Silas Marner** *by George Eliot*

But it doesn't always have to be happy.

*Day had dawned. It was the fourth day. Now everything was lost, but they would not surrender ...*

*Here on the roof of a public-house, in a narrow slum street, the two men waited, waited for death. It was terrible ...*

*Silence ... a long silence. All was still.*

*Then there were footsteps on the roof behind him. He heard them and jumped up, waving his arms above his head. Then he fell on his knees and bent forward chattering and fluttering his clawing hands.*

*'Take me out of this. Take me out of this. I didn't fire. I didn't fire. He was mad. My wife, my wife. I declare to God I never fired. Two men on the stairs. Murphy is his name. Take me out of this.'*

*There were two of them there, peering over the ridge of the roof, five feet away from his face. Only their faces, their arms and their rifles were visible. Two cruel, cold faces, staring coldly at him. Gradually he saw the faces growing colder and more cruel, the lips curling into a snarl and the eyes narrowing. Then one man said: 'Let's give it to the bastard.'*

*Then they both fired point blank into his head.*

From **Civil War** by Liam O' Flaherty

## EXAM TIP

Do not have a clichéd ending. Almost anything is better than: 'Then I woke up. It had all been a dream.'

## TASK

1   Make out a plot line for a short story, using the following pattern:

■   introduction – paragraph 1

■   build-up/development – paragraphs 2–5

■   climax – paragraphs 6 and 7

■   conclusion/resolution – paragraph 8.

Then decide which type of ending you will give it: a cliffhanger, a twist in the tale or a resolution.

2   Write the concluding paragraph.

### SAMPLE SHORT STORY

'I'm glad to see you,' I replied.

**Write a short story suggested by these words.**

1   *The cold November evening hurtled round me. It was pitch dark and I found it hard to see in front of me. I held a bottle of orange tightly in my hand. My phone was securely hidden in my pocket, just in case. I glanced over my shoulder, sure*

*I had heard footsteps. But there was no-one to be seen. I hurried to Anne's gate and ran briskly up the driveway, the tall evergreens swaying frantically in the deepening gloom. I rang the door-bell and after what seemed a lifetime, there was Anne. Grinning cheerfully, she pulled me in.*

*'Are you OK? You look as if you've seen a ghost,' she laughed.*

*'No, I'm fine,' I answered somewhat shakily.*

*'Imagining things as usual,' Anne grinned.*

2   *Well, Friday had arrived again, and all the gang were here for our weekly meeting. The topics would be the usual ... who fancied whom, the hated maths teacher, spots, shoes, etc., etc. The sitting room was a kaleidoscope of colour ... popcorn, sweets, crisps and mineral bottles lay in glorious heaps. A great fire roared orange and red up the chimney. My previous misgivings seemed very foolish. I plopped down on a floor cushion and Anne popped in a movie. Someone dimmed the lights.*

3   *'This is supposed to be scary, anyone who screams has to pay a forfeit,' Anne teased. We all laughed loudly. But after ten minutes there was petrified silence. We clung to the cushions unable to look. I was petrified. Bang! Suddenly the room was plunged into total darkness. Everyone was screaming and bumping into each other in the dark. Mad black figures silhouetted against the roaring fire.*

4   *I sat frozen to the spot. I was back to a place I never want to visit. Two years ago, on a similar night to this, Anne and Julie and I were walking home from the cinema, chatting happily. I lived just 100 yards in the opposite direction to the pair.*

*'I'll be fine,' I insisted. 'It's only a hen's race home.'*

*'If you're sure,' Anne replied.*

*'Yeah, go on, I'm no scaredy cat,' I reassured her.*

*'Well, text us as you go along for the craic,' Anne said.*

5   *Off the pair went and were quickly hidden from view in the foggy night. The street seemed eerily quiet. I took out my new mobile and groaned in disbelief. I was out of credit. I started to walk quickly and suddenly I became aware of an echoing pair of footsteps. I quickened my pace. The footsteps quickened too. I stopped. The footsteps stopped too. I looked around and felt a tight grip on my neck.*

6   *'Empty your pockets!' the figure hissed.*

*I fumbled for the twenty euro note. The note and my phone were grabbed roughly. Suddenly I felt my head making contact with the hard pavement and then I knew no more ...*

7   *Plop! Suddenly I was woken by a drop of rain sliding off a leaf above. My eyes opened. My arm and leg ached. I didn't know where I was. The fog swirled menacingly. Two figures appeared. I tried to scream.*

*'Hey, it's only us,' Anne said. 'Did you fall? What happened? Can you stand?'*

8   *I could only lie there, unable to move or speak ... Blackness descended. And now here I was frozen as before. A spark flew out from the fire and quickly caught on the heaps of coloured paper lying about. The room soon became a furnace as cushions, curtains and debris caught fire. Thick black smoke began to envelop the room. I watched as if it had nothing to do with me. Suddenly I saw Anne silhouetted against the roaring flames.*

9   *'Rose, are you there?' she screamed, desperately. Suddenly there was a crash. A light fitting fell on Anne and she crumpled to the ground. I was beside her in a flash. I tried to get her arm but it just fell away. I started to choke on the thick smoke coming from the burning furniture. My eyes were smarting and streaming. But Anne had been there for me. I had to do what I could. I hauled and dragged her into the hall, holding my jumper to my mouth to avoid inhaling the stench-filled smoke. Anne was heavy and the hall seemed endless. I did not seem to be making much progress, but I remembered that night, two years ago, when Anne had bravely stayed with me while Julie ran off for help, and I started to pull again ... My arms ached and there was a deep pain in my chest. Just when I thought I would not be able to go on, I saw a fireman's helmet and I knew we were safe.*

10  *Next day, we awoke beside each other in hospital. We grinned ruefully at each other.*

*'I'm glad to see you,' Anne whispered, bandaged like an Egyptian mummy.*

*'I'm glad to see you too,' I replied, waving my one unrestricted finger.*

*(840 words)*

GRADE: A2

P = 26/30

C = 25/30

L = 26/30

M = 9/10

Total = 86%

*The Shared Dream of Storytelling*

*by Maeve Binchy*

*Well, of course the Irish have a long and honourable tradition of storytelling. Before the invention of printing brought books into our homes, we had Seanchaí (storytellers) wandering from home to home. They were warmly welcomed and treated with great respect as they came to castle and cottage. They were wined and dined, and neighbours flocked in to hear their tales. Nobody warned each other that boring old Seanchaí were in the neighbourhood and everyone should lie low. Having escaped entirely the Victorian edict in England that we should not speak until spoken to, the Irish love a story. And the only thing better than listening to one is telling one. So, it's there in the national psyche, telling stories.*

# Maeve Binchy's Top Writing Tips

- write what you know and care about. That way you will be an expert in your field
- write as you speak, using phrases as if talking to a friend. Don't show off
- use your eyes and ears as if they were a camera and tape recorder. This will teach you to be observant
- it's always much easier to tell other people what to do rather than sit down and do it. And oddly, in a world obsessed with exercise and workouts, writing has a lot to do with sitting down and not getting up until it is finished. Let's get down to it.

# CHAPTER 15
# NARRATIVE AND THE AESTHETIC USE OF LANGUAGE

Language can be used as an artistic medium to give pleasure, excite our imaginations and reveal insights about our world. This has always been associated with poetry, drama and fiction, but it can be argued that every kind of good appropriate writing involves the aesthetic use of language.

This is the opening section of a well-known American novel.

*It happened that green and crazy summer when Frankie was twelve years old. This was the summer when for a long time she had not been a member. She belonged to no club and was a member of nothing in the world. Frankie had become an unjoined person who hung around in doorways, and she was afraid. In June the trees were bright dizzy green, but later the leaves darkened, and the town turned black and shrunken under the glare of the sun. At first Frankie walked around doing one thing and another. The sidewalks finally became too hot for Frankie's feet, and also she got herself in trouble. She was in so much secret trouble that she thought it was better to stay at home – and at home there was only Berenice Sadie Brown and John Henry West. The three of them sat at the kitchen table, saying the same things over and over, so that by August the words began to rhyme with each other and sound strange. The world seemed to die each afternoon and nothing moved any longer. At last the summer was like a green sick dream, or like a silent crazy jungle under glass. And then, on the last Friday of August, all this was changed: it was so sudden that Frankie puzzled the whole blank afternoon, and still she did not understand.*

From **The Member of the Wedding** *by Carson McCullers*

In addition to raising questions about what had changed, we begin to get a glimpse inside the mind of a child who is caught between the yearning to belong and the urge to run away.

The extract below is an evocative description of a city at night.

*Car lights reflecting and flashing off the wet road; tyres swishing through the pools of standing water; young people out for the evening dodging the spray and giggling happily with their friends. That is the city most of you see, but I keep to the side streets and alleyways where I hope to find a dry, warm spot for the night. Here's an air vent from a restaurant: warm gusts of air laden with the aromas and spices from the exotic east ... no dinner for me tonight, unless I'm lucky. Past a noisy backstreet pub now; everyone shouting – singing, maybe – and more lights and smells. Dustbin lids falling nearby; perhaps it's another homeless person like me, or a cat on the prowl. I saw a fox once, vivid, brown-red against a white shop wall, tearing a rubbish bag to pieces. Rubbish is everywhere. They put it out at night, great stacks of it waiting for the bin lorries which carry on their work all night long. They say the city never sleeps, and they're right ...*

This vivid description shows some originality by being written through the eyes of someone who sleeps rough at night. Images are precise and detailed, creating an edgy atmosphere. There are some interesting sentence structures and the use of present tense verbs adds an air of drama to the scene.

In this example, Alice Walker describes her memories of her mother.

*Whatever she planted grew as if by magic, and her fame as a grower of flowers spread over three counties. Because of her creativity with her flowers, even my memories of poverty are seen through a screen of blooms – sunflowers, petunias, roses, dahlias, forsythia, spirea, delphiniums, verbena ... and on and on.*

*And I remember people coming to my mother's yard to be given cuttings from her flowers; I hear again the praise showered on her because whatever rocky soil she landed on, she turned into a garden. A garden so brilliant with colours, so original in its design, so magnificent with life and creativity, that to this day people drive by our house in Georgia – perfect strangers and imperfect strangers – and ask to stand or walk among my mother's art.*

*I notice that it is only when my mother is working in her flowers that she is radiant, almost to the point of being invisible – except as Creator: hand and eye. She is involved in work her soul must have. Ordering the universe in the image of her personal conception of Beauty.*

*From **In Search of Our Mothers' Gardens** by Alice Walker*

Throughout this extract, the writer associates her mother with the beauty and skills of gardening. Indeed, it seems as though gardening is a symbol of her mother's life. Instead of speaking in an obvious way about her feelings, imaginative writing like this is much more interesting. Alice Walker is also the author of *The Color Purple*.

## SAMPLE ESSAY

A Child of Our Time

**Write a short story about the life and music of a young person living in Ireland today.**

1   *Vanessa had been in and out of psychiatric care for most of her young life. The usual 'bad family background'. By the age of seventeen, she had already been in juvenile prison on two separate occasions. Shortly after the last shoplifting case, she began carving her body. In a way it was to get back at her mother. She also loved the sense of the rush of blood to her head as she used the knife on her arm. Vanessa would try anything. She dabbled in drink and drugs of all kinds. Boyfriends came and went. There were a number of suicide attempts, some half-hearted, others serious attempts to end her miserable life.*

2   *Today, Vanessa works for a national tabloid newspaper and part of her work is to report on how young people spend their free time. Here she tells the story of her visit behind the scenes to a rave party held in one of Dublin's top entertainment venues.*

3   *It's three o'clock in the afternoon and I embrace myself as I go undercover to check out the Cellar. Security is tight at the entrance as the big men in suits give brief body searches to the scantily-clad clubbers arriving. Giggling groups of young teens race by me to skip the queue. I look at my ticket again to make sure. It reads 'Over-18s Only'. Identification isn't an issue at the door. Everyone who turns up gets in. As always, the gardai are too busy looking out for the ecstasy pushers.*

4   *Although the pounding music hurts my ears, the first thing I really notice is a mass of jutting jaws and bulging eyes. Within minutes, someone asks me 'Fancy a disco biscuit, love?' I push my way through the half-naked sweating bodies and notice a handmade poster on a wall outside the toilets. 'XTC – Come Up and Come Down!' Close by, two smiling youths sell plastic bottles of water at €5-a-pop.*

5   *Inside the toilets are crowds of pill-filled girls waiting to empty their bladders. They squeeze their tiny bodies into cubicles in twos and threes. Some of them are singing and shouting. One is sitting in a corner crying. A white-faced girl stares at me and says something which I can't really hear because of the noise. I think she's asking me for money but I'm afraid to get involved. She seems stone cold and her pupils are dark and enlarged. She disappears and I keep thinking that she is exactly like I was just a few years ago.*

6   *Later on, I watch the scene in the dance area. Most of the dancers are in a trance and are totally into the music. At least five guys approach me asking if I need a 'top-up'. One young clubber shouts in my ear that his heart has been taken over by the beat. Others mouth obscenities when I turn them down. Two guys dance back to back together. One bends over forwards and the other leans back on him, their two spines in line. Someone shouts 'Back breaker!' and points at the two lads. She tells me that when you're on E, the nerves along your spinal chord become almost electrified. 'You feel great,' she explains. 'Pure class.'*

7   *I make my way to The Cellar's 'chill zone' where everyone is either coming up or coming down. You have to almost gasp for breath here. The sawdust-covered carpets have become beds and couches for the dozens of couples clawing at each other's bodies. There is no shame any more. The stench of*

*vomit turns my stomach. Down beside the exit door, a group of youths urinate against a wall. No one stares. No one takes any notice. Up on the balconies, I find the VIP area.*

8  *You're supposed to have a special pass, but the security guard asks me for my phone number instead. I walk in to the noise and chaos of a spaced-out couple jumping on chairs, whistles in their mouths and arms in the air. One guy is slumped in a corner trying to use a syringe – heroin, I presume. Three or four other lads are fighting and arguing among themselves. Other young males lie collapsed around the room. It's almost five o'clock in the afternoon. One guy is being woken up by two security men. They help him stand up. He gets to his feet but soon collapses again. They don't bother him a second time.*

9  *Overcome by noise and the clammy air, I sit down between bare thighs and fluffy Eskimo boots. Drunken chanting surrounds me. Every so often, someone asks me if I'm on 'a good buzz'. One couple talk to me. The girl is on her third E, her boyfriend on his fifth. Her ears, nose and lips are pierced. 'I take dope because I want to die happy,' her boyfriend says. Beads of sweat dribble down from his shaved head. He boasts about his overdoses and tells me that he had to have his stomach pumped a month earlier. 'Welcome to Ireland!' he laughs.*

10  *For some unknown reason, I start to think of how I might have turned out if I had not changed my life in time. Then I remember something I read in a poetry class many years ago – 'Hope is the thing with feathers that perches on the soul.'*

GRADE: A1

P = 30/30

C = 30/30

L = 30/30

M = 10/10

Total = 100%

## EXAMINER'S COMMENT

This narrative is a good example of the aesthetic use of language. The story is well structured and the writer succeeds in creating the edgy atmosphere of the club's interior by describing various scenes and characters in some detail. Paragraphs 6 and 9 are particularly effective. Short sentences and the use of the present tense add to the dramatic mood. The ending successfully brings our attention back to the narrator and her own memories.

## TASKS

1   Choose one example of effective descriptive writing from the essay and briefly explain why it caught your attention.

2   Replace paragraph 10 by writing your own alternative ending to the story.

## EXAM TIP

When writing a short story prompted by one or more of the visual images you are given, it is important to let the examiner know that you are actually linking your narrative to the photograph (or photographs) and not simply re-hashing a 'prepared story' that has little or nothing to do with the pictures.

# PRACTICE QUESTIONS: COMPOSING

Write a composition on **any one** of the following.

Each composition carries 100 marks.

The composition assignments below are intended to reflect language study in the areas of information, argument, persuasion, narration and the aesthetic use of language.

## A Teenage Life

1 'That's the good thing about friends.'

Write an article for your school magazine explaining what your friends mean to you. (You may use a diary format if you wish.)

2 'They're all the same!'

Write a serious argument in which you argue for or against the stereotyping of teenagers in modern society.

3 'If only I knew then what I know now.'

Write a personal essay or short story suggested by the above sentence.

4 'Are you really going out in **that**?'

Write an article (serious or humorous) for a teenage magazine in which you express your personal views on young people's fashion.

5 'It's good to write.'

Write a letter (or a series of letters) to a pen-friend in which you describe your experiences selecting a college course or choosing a career.

6 'Travel light, travel right.'

Write a newspaper article aimed at young people in which you give advice to teenagers intending to go abroad on a school trip or a summer holiday.

7 Write a short story suggested by one or more of the images on page 113.

## B Sport

1 'The weekend wouldn't be the same without it.'

Write an article, intended for a popular newspaper or magazine, in which you outline your views on the GAA.

2 'A healthy mind in a healthy body.'

Write an address aimed at school parents in which you urge them to encourage their children to take part in PE classes and school sports.

3   'No time for losers.'

Write a personal essay that explores the idea of competition in sport.

4   'The love of sport seems to be in our blood.'

Write an informative magazine article with the title: 'Ireland – A Great Sporting Nation'.

5   'Some people think football is a matter of life and death ... I can assure them it's much more serious than that.'

You are a dedicated fan of one of the world's great football teams. Write your story. Your composition may take the form of a series of diary entries if you wish.

6   'These are the heroes of the beautiful game.'

Write a newspaper article in which you try to persuade readers of the importance of sports stars in our lives.

7   Write a short story suggested by one or more of the sporting images on page 114.

# C Environment

1   'That's what pollution does.'

Write a speech you would give to your classmates about the importance of environmental responsibility.

2   'If a good God made the world, why has it gone wrong?'

Write an article for a local newspaper, giving your thoughts on this question.

3   'We are a fast-changing society and change is always threatening to some of us.'

Write a persuasive composition that addresses this issue.

4   'Sometimes I don't know whether to laugh or cry.'

You and your family have recently come from another country to live in Ireland. Write a journal (or diary) expressing your thoughts and feelings about your new surroundings and the people you meet.

5   'A toxic food environment.'

Write an informative essay in response to this title.

6   'A tin box on wheels is beginning to make life unbearable.'

Write an argumentative essay on the problem of traffic congestion and what should be done about it.

7   Write a short story suggested by one or more of the images on page 115.

# D Conflict

1 'Like everyone else, I thought it could never happen to me.'

Imagine that you have been the victim of a serious crime. Write a first-person account of your experience.

2 'Ireland is becoming an increasingly racist society.'

This is the topic for your next school debate. Write the speech you would make either against or in favour of this motion.

3 'I suppose I have only myself to blame.'

Imagine you are a prisoner currently serving a sentence for violent disorder. Compose a series of diary entries in which you reflect on your past crimes and present lifestyle.

4 'It can be stopped!'

Write an article aimed at a magazine for young adult readers in which you draw attention to the issue of bullying in secondary schools.

5 'How are we to explain all the harm done in the name of religion?'

In an article intended for publication in your local newspaper, give your own thoughts on this question.

6 'It happens every day.'

Write a serious newspaper article in which you argue for or against the need to have a stricter system of law and order.

7 Write a short story suggested by one or more of the images on page 116.

# A Teenage Life

# Sport

# Environment

# Conflict

# SECTION 3
# LITERARY ESSAYS

Paper 2 (Literature) gives students a wonderful opportunity to enjoy a wide range of texts. With so much drama, film, fiction and poetry to study, reading and language development can really come alive.

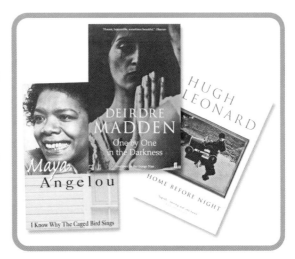

The aim of this part of the book is to offer general guidelines on tackling the various questions on Paper 2. Every year, there are more than fifty authors to choose from. Different class groups will pick whatever combinations of texts interest them most.

This final section includes useful suggestions to help you approach the various questions in Paper 2 and offers helpful advice on writing successful literary essays. Practice questions, examiners' comments and sample essays will also refine your exam technique.

You will be required to write three **literary essays** for Leaving Certificate English Higher Level Paper 2.

- Section I – the **Single Text**. Candidates have one hour to write about a play or novel they have studied
- Section II – the **Comparative Study** offers a choice of questions – either one 70-minute essay or two shorter ones
- Section III – **Poetry**. This includes one 50-minute essay on one of the prescribed poets.

As always, the most important piece of advice about writing a critical essay is simply to **answer the question**. Even if the essay is the right length, shows knowledge of the text and is well expressed, it will not be successful if it does not **focus** on what the question is asking you to do.

Therefore, the starting point of your essay should **not** be the text you have studied, but the **question** you are answering.

# Planning the Essay

Once you have looked closely at the wording of the question and clarified in your mind what the question is asking you to do, you should jot down some preliminary notes to organise your ideas. While it is tempting not to bother doing this, a few minutes spent planning your essay will save you time later on.

You should have a clear idea of how the essay is going to develop.

You don't have to write out anything in detail; the briefest of headings will do. Your planning notes are for your use only and might well be rather messy, with words scored out and arrows used to change the order of points. However, five minutes or so spent planning will help you avoid the following difficulties:

- mentioning all the things that first come into your mind and then running out of ideas
- remembering points you should have made earlier
- drifting away from the approach you started off with in the introduction.

# Using Quotations

Short, relevant quotations are essential in good literary essays.

Remember to **quote effectively**:

- place inverted commas at the beginning and end of the quotation
- write the quotation exactly as it was in the original text
- avoid using a quotation that repeats something you have just written
- try to work the quote into your own sentence.

Ideally, quotations should be carefully chosen to support or illustrate a point you are making. For example:

*In Charles Dickens' novel, **Great Expectations**, the fact that Estella embarrasses Pip by referring to his 'thick boots' and 'coarse hands' shows us how cruel and insensitive she is.*

When using longer quotations, take a new line and indent (as for a new paragraph) to show the quoted section.

*Emily Dickinson creates a disturbing effect when describing her isolated soul as:*

> *'And I, and Silence, some strange Race*
> *Wrecked Solitary – here – '*

*Early on in the play, Macbeth makes it clear that he is a fearless soldier:*

> *'I dare do all that may become a man;*
> *Who dares do more is none.'*

In these examples, the quotations make points and add to our understanding. The words used by the poet Emily Dickinson highlight her deep sense of loneliness. In Macbeth's case, we know that he is a proud man. His great confidence is plainly seen in the quotation above.

## TASK

Using your own Single Text, name a main character and one of his/her qualities. Write a sentence **incorporating a key quotation** to illustrate this particular quality.

# Beginning the Essay

It is important to focus on the question from the very first sentence. Don't take a roundabout approach, such as giving a short account of the story. Instead, you should summarise the line of argument you intend to follow in the essay.

## SAMPLE OPENING PARAGRAPHS

**The enduring genius of Shakespeare is that he creates tragic heroes about whom we care. In your view, how true is this statement in relation to the character of Hamlet? Support your answer by reference to the text.**

An opening paragraph might be:

> *From the opening scenes of Shakespeare's play, we sympathise with Hamlet because of the difficult position he finds himself in after his father's death. The young prince is first seen as an isolated character who is already suspicious of Claudius, the new king. Shakespeare goes on to use frequent soliloquies to show how Hamlet struggles to take revenge against his uncle. This helps us to see things from Hamlet's point of view and increases our understanding of his tortured personality.*

Note that the opening paragraph should be short and general in its approach. Indeed, the introduction should be a summary of the whole essay.

**Miss Havisham's obsession with revenge makes her the most pathetic figure in *Great Expectations*. Discuss this view, supporting your points by reference to Dickens' novel.**

*We first see Miss Havisham in her gloomy home, Satis House, which she has deliberately allowed to fall into bad repair because of the disappointment of her wedding day. Her bitterness is clearly seen as she humiliates Pip repeatedly. From the outset, she is a pathetic character, trapped in the past and filled with one single obsession – to take revenge on all men for the wrong done to her by one man. Throughout the story, she torments herself by refusing to come to terms with her disappointment. In her pitiful selfishness, Miss Havisham uses Estella as part of her revenge and wastes her own life in trying to destroy the lives of those around her.*

Note how this opening paragraph goes straight to the main aspects mentioned in the question, making reference to the key words: 'obsession', 'revenge' and 'pathetic'.

## TASK

Write a similar introductory paragraph for one of the Single Text questions in your past papers. Exchange your attempts with a partner and discuss their strengths or/and weaknesses.

Remember that a **successful introduction** will:

- focus on the question straightaway
- refer to key words from the question
- outline the argument to be presented in the rest of the essay.

## EXAM TIP

- whichever text you have studied, play or novel, you will be expected to show a clear knowledge and understanding of it. The examiner will be looking for evidence that you are able to **analyse the text**
- there will be a choice of questions, so pick the one that suits you best and **plan your main points** very carefully, ensuring that you have **relevant references and quotations** to support them
- **study the wording of the question** to make certain that you understand what you need to focus on in your answer. Many questions ask you to do two or more distinct things, and omitting one of these immediately reduces your marks
- **avoid writing a mere summary** of the story. Instead, use the story to support key points that address the question.

# CHAPTER 16
# SINGLE TEXT GUIDELINES

## Single Text Theme Questions

All texts deal with interesting aspects of human experience. Authors create new realities for us. Themes are ideas or issues explored in texts. Love is a central theme in many stories, such as Shakespeare's *King Lear*. But this play also deals with other themes, including ingratitude, justice, power, violence and redemption.

It is always of interest to see how a writer or film director presents a theme, and whether the treatment of a theme affects our understanding of it.

At the very least, authors give us a glimpse of how others see the world. We read texts and watch films to find out more about what it is like to be a human being, not to be told how to be one. The characters and themes in Single Texts should be explored in detail.

Common themes include:

- relationships
- conflict
- love and/or friendship
- change
- power
- revenge
- appearance and reality
- ambition
- escapism
- pride
- disorder
- tragedy
- fate
- good and evil.

## EXAM TIP

When planning your answer, consider the following:

- is a particular theme of central importance in the text?
- or is it really a sub-theme?
- when does the reader first become aware of the theme?
- which scenes or moments really focus on the theme?
- what aspects of the theme are explored?
- what point is the author making about the theme?
- do we understand the theme more at the end of the story?
- was the theme treated in an interesting way?
- what have we learned about it?

### SAMPLE ANSWER

**Discuss the role and significance of kingship as a theme in Shakespeare's play, *Macbeth*. Support the points you make by close reference to the play. (Textual support may include reference to a particular performance of the play that you have seen on stage or film.)**

Possible points for consideration:

- kingship in the sixteenth century
- the obsessive ambition of Macbeth and his wife
- Macbeth's reaction after killing Duncan
- the king's relationship with his people
- the views of Macduff and Malcolm
- Macbeth's final thoughts on his misrule
- Shakespeare's views on imperial power
- the imagery and symbolism of kingship.

1   *Kingship and the pursuit of it is a major theme in many of Shakespeare's plays. In Macbeth, we see that kingship is a central theme around which the whole story revolves. In Shakespeare's time, the king of a country was seen as a divine appointment who had absolute power and was expected to guide and protect his people. This play presents us with three different kings, Duncan, Macbeth and Malcolm. By contrasting these three, Shakespeare gives us a better understanding of what kingship means.*

2   *The first image of royal power we see is King Duncan. It is immediately apparent that his reign has been neither peaceful nor successful. We first see Duncan on the battlefield, receiving news about how his own army has defeated the rebel Thane of Cawdor and MacDonwald. Even at this early stage, we can see a growing sense of uneasiness about Duncan's position as King. We also learn that Scotland is being invaded by armies from Norway. It is clear that Duncan is under attack from many sides. At the execution of Cawdor, we find out the reason why his reign has been blighted by war. After Cawdor's death, the king remarks: 'He was a gentleman on whom I built an absolute trust.' But Duncan does not learn from his mistake. He is to repeat it again with Macbeth, resulting in fatal consequences. We can see that the 'golden round' is a poisoned chalice.*

3   *Throughout the play, the crown is a symbol for Scotland's decline into violence and terror. We can see how strong and powerful the attraction of kingship is. It proves to be the reason for the transformation of Macbeth from a brave and loyal hero to a merciless 'butcher'. The words of the witches coupled with pressure from Lady Macbeth help to persuade Macbeth to give in to his one fatal flaw – ambition. Because of his obsession with the kingship, he has been reduced from being 'valour's minion' to stabbing an old man 'who hath borne his faculties so meek' while he slept. The tragedy is that Macbeth could have been a noble king. Unfortunately for him and everyone in Scotland, he allowed his 'black and deep desires' to win.*

4   *To the people of Scotland, Macbeth becomes a cruel, calculating tyrant. The audience, however, can see the inner turmoil that being king has brought to Macbeth. He is overcome by guilt immediately after the murder and soon becomes steeped in paranoia. These insecurities cause him to order the murder of Banquo, the attempted murder of Fleance and the needless massacre of Macduff's family. The deep desire to be king brought Macbeth into a fast descent into a violent world of corruption. We can see that this is a far cry from the respected position he once held. It is ironic that becoming king robbed Macbeth of his honour, his sanity and ultimately his life.*

5   *By concentrating on Macbeth's evil reign, Shakespeare shows us how the whole country reflects the type of king who is in power. Macbeth's deceit and corruption quickly spreads throughout all of Scotland. He has never been a natural leader who put his people first. His disgraceful behaviour has led to him having spies in every part of the land. He himself mixes with murderers and relies on the witches for advice. Under the rule of this hated dictator, Macduff sums up Macbeth's reign: 'Each new morn, new widows howl, new orphans cry.' It is clear that power has corrupted Macbeth and turned him into an inhuman tyrant. This is the exact opposite of what a king should be.*

6   *Our third image of kingship is Malcolm, son of Duncan and rightful heir to the throne. Unlike Macbeth, personal ambition is not so important to him. He seems to have a genuine love for his people and wishes to rid Scotland of Macbeth's evil. Perhaps he is the best kind of king. He is much more careful with people, and a better judge of his colleagues. We learn how hard it is to be a successful king. Both Duncan and Macbeth failed in different ways. However, Malcolm embodies some of the traits or 'graces' he discussed with Macduff when they spoke about the character of a good king:*

> *'justice, verity, temperance, stableness,*
>
> *bounty, perseverance, mercy, lowliness,*
>
> *devotion, patience, courage, fortitude'.*

7   *Shakespeare tells us the qualities needed by a king and Malcolm seems better equipped than anybody else to face the challenges that go hand in hand with ruling Scotland. He does not trust so easily, but still has a high regard for loyalty. We can see this when he tests Macduff's loyalty to Scotland. At the end of the play, the role of the king, which had been tainted with bloodshed and deceit, is now in the hands of someone who can fulfil the ideals of a true ruler. We can see that a proper king needs to have high standards if he is to rule a country well.*

8   *It can be argued that kingship plays an extremely significant role in Shakespeare's Macbeth. We can see the way a king's character accounts for the way he rules a country. Duncan is a well-meaning man, but he seems weak. In Macbeth's case, it is from his 'devilish' obsession with personal power and kingship that all the deceit, bloodshed and tragedy stem. The three kings we see in the play show us how power can either be used properly or abused. The characters of Duncan, Macbeth and Malcolm are clearly seen in the way they act as kings of Scotland. Shakespeare concentrates on one corrupt king who took over the throne by evil means and who soon brought about tragedy in his country and for himself.*

GRADE: A1

P = 18/18

C = 18/18

L = 18/18

M = 6/6

Total = 60/60

## EXAMINER'S COMMENT

This was a good intelligent response to a typically general theme question. It included a wide range of references and focused well on the political implications of kingship.

The second-last paragraph is an effective one, bringing together the ideals needed in a true king. Although the phrase 'we can see' was over-used, the overall expression was controlled and points were clearly made throughout.

## TASKS

1   Go through the sample essay carefully to see how many times the phrase: 'we can see' was used. Suggest four alternative phrases.

2   With reference to your own Single Text, write down short answers to the following questions:

 (a) What themes (if any) are suggested by the title of your set text?

 (b) Describe a key scene where an important theme is apparent.

 (c) Write down two or three interesting quotes from this scene that help to illustrate this theme. Briefly explain what each quote adds to our understanding of the theme.

 (d) What insights do the characters gain at the end of the text?

 (e) What have you learned about the theme from this scene?

## ASSIGNMENT

Using this sample as a model answer, choose an important theme that is central to the text you are studying and write a timed essay (60 minutes) about the significance of the theme in your text.

# Responding to Questions on Character

Questions on the set text often require you to respond to a main character in the story. In fiction, authors use different ways to create and reveal characters. In the examples that follow, Emily Brontë, the author of *Wuthering Heights*, describes the young Heathcliff.

## Telling

*He seemed a sullen, patient child; hardened, perhaps to ill-treatment.*

This is explicit information. The reader is being told what to think about the character.

## Showing

The writer can show us what a character is like through appearance, action, speech (or lack of speech), and also through the use of setting.

Writers often use appearance to suggest character. The effect on the reader depends on the choice of vocabulary – which may be positive or negative.

*I had a peep at a dirty, ragged, black-haired child: big enough to walk and talk; indeed its face looked older than Catherine's.*

The writer can describe the behaviour of the character and let the reader form a judgement about the character based on what he or she does.

*Yet when it was set on its feet, it only stared around, and repeated over and over again some gibberish, nobody could understand.*

In both these cases the reader has to infer. The writer does not tell us explicitly that Heathcliff was a very strange individual even as a child.

Another way authors can create characters is to let the reader judge them from what they say. Here we see the violence in Heathcliff.

*'I'd not exchange for a thousand lives, my condition here, for Edgar Linton's at Thrushcross Grange – not if I might have the privilege of flinging Joseph off the highest gable, and painting the house front with Hindley's blood.'*

An author might use setting to show what happens to a character when he is constantly exposed to bad influences.

*One may guess at the power of the north wind blowing over the edge, by the excessive slant of a few stunted firs at the end of the house.*

# Character Profile

Take the main character in your set text and **make a quick profile** of him or her by noting:

- what the character does – or fails to do (inner conflict)
- what the character says (or fails to say), and how
- what motivates the character (goal)
- how the character is dressed
- how the character feels or does not feel
- what other characters think and say about your chosen character (admire/dislike)
- what changes occur in the character (new insight)
- what the author tells us directly about the character (omniscient point of view).

Some useful phrases for describing a character. He or she:

- is presented as ...
- is portrayed as ...
- is revealed as ...
- is shaped as ...
- comes across as ...
- strikes us as ...
- appears to be ...
- emerges as ...

## EXAM TIP

When two characters are contrasted in a play or story, we usually watch to see how they relate or react to each other. This creates dramatic interest. In preparing for the Single Text question, study at least two key scenes in depth. Choose scenes that are turning points in the narrative. Most Leaving Cert questions will allow for discussion of important scenes where main characters reveal themselves or where the drama is compelling.

## SAMPLE ANSWER

Everything that happens in the novel *Wuthering Heights* is centred on the character of Heathcliff. Discuss this view of the novel, supporting the points you make by reference to the text.

Possible points for consideration:

- Heathcliff makes an immediate impact on the Earnshaw family
- he completely transforms Cathy's life
- his cruel ways are a shocking and compelling element of the story
- he gains control of both Wuthering Heights and Thrushcross Grange
- he stands out in contrast to weaker characters
- readers are left with a powerful impression of Heathcliff.

But:

- Cathy Earnshaw is a driving force for Heathcliff
- his influence fades away towards the end
- readers become more interested in the younger characters.

1  *I would fully agree that* **Wuthering Heights** *centres on the character of Heathcliff. Without him, there would hardly be a story. It is very likely that most readers would have a love-hate relationship with Heathcliff, many of them unable to decide on whether he is a hero or a villain. But he is certainly the one character we all associate with this story. Heathcliff is the centre of attention from beginning to end. He affects every other character and destroys the lives of many of them.*

2  *Our reaction to Heathcliff is one of disdain and disgust as well as compassion and sympathy. This is Emily Brontë's great triumph. We feel most sympathy for Heathcliff at the start of the novel when old Mr Earnshaw brings home this dark homeless orphan from the back streets of Liverpool. But from the moment he arrived, Heathcliff 'bred ill feeling' and was greatly resented by Hindley who was angry that Heathcliff was Mr Earnshaw's favourite. For a short while, the family referred to the dark orphan boy as 'it'.*

3   As Heathcliff settles into the Heights, he dominates the lives of those around
    him. In some ways, he shows himself to be manipulative, for example in the
    incident with the colts. Mr Earnshaw had given Hindley and Heathcliff two
    colts, and Heathcliff had chosen the finer one. But when his horse went lame,
    he demanded that Hindley hand over his. The boys fought and Hindley struck
    Heathcliff with an iron bar. This gave Heathcliff the opportunity to blackmail
    Hindley who was afraid that his father, Mr Earnshaw, would find out. This
    was a good example of how Heathcliff began to control others. As a result,
    readers can see his dark, evil side.

4   Already we can see how Heathcliff begins to shape Hindley's life. Hindley
    develops an obsession with Heathcliff and becomes bitter about Heathcliff's
    place in the family. Even though Cathy disliked him at first, they soon grew
    very 'thick'. In time, their relationship became stronger, especially under
    Hindley's tyrannical rage. After he had been degraded by Hindley, Heathcliff
    and Cathy spent their days rambling on the moors together. The really
    memorable scenes in the story are all concerned with Heathcliff, such as the
    time when he and Cathy spy on the Linton children. Once again, Emily
    Brontë shapes the story around Heathcliff and makes the reader feel sorry
    for him.

5   It is also worth noting that Nelly Dean only begins her story from the day
    Heathcliff arrives in Wuthering Heights. Everything changed that day. After
    all the passion and revenge, Heathcliff eventually causes Cathy's death. She
    had always struggled between her feelings for him and Edgar. After hearing
    her say that 'it would degrade me to marry Heathcliff', he leaves the Heights.
    It is worth noting that Nelly goes into no detail about life at Wuthering
    Heights until he returns as a 'gentleman' some years later. This shows that all
    the important parts of the story involve Heathcliff.

6   After he returns, Heathcliff really dominates the whole story. Because he seeks
    revenge on all those he sees as enemies – Hindley, Edgar, Hareton and
    Isabella, he becomes the focal point of the novel. He is more mysterious than
    ever, and we can only guess that he has been in the army. In a short while, he
    encourages Hindley's alcoholism and wins the Heights from Hindley in a
    game of cards. The reader is bound to wonder just how evil Heathcliff has
    become. For example, does he want Hindley to drink himself to death?

7   Heathcliff's bitterness over losing Cathy dominates the story. After Hindley's
    death, Heathcliff turns his attention to young Hareton, saying, 'Now you are
    mine. And let's see if one tree won't grow as crooked as the other, with the
    same wind to twist it.' He degrades Hareton just as he was degraded.
    Strangely, despite the terrible treatment, Hareton still has some affection for

*his tormentor. This makes us wonder about Heathcliff even more, and we ask ourselves why he has such power over others. However, it is Isabella above all who notices Heathcliff's devilish qualities. She sees him as 'half-man, half fiend'. As part of his revenge, he marries her and treats her infernally, saying that he will beat her every day.*

8   *Throughout all this, Heathcliff remains Cathy's hero. Her love for him is still resembles 'the eternal rocks beneath, a source of little visible light, but necessary'. His obsessive love for her allows him to show his softer, more human qualities. He treats Cathy differently from everyone else and allows the reader to warm to him as Cathy falls ill and close to death. Their love story grips our attention. Cathy's death is dramatic and overwhelming. Like everything else in this story, it has all come about because of Heathcliff's arrival at the Heights.*

9   *While Heathcliff is the single most important character in the novel, Catherine Earnshaw is also a leading figure who shares some of the limelight with him. Most readers think of these two unhappy lovers running free across the wild moors, a symbol of their uncontrolled relationship. But even Catherine admits that she is being led by the man she loves when she says 'Nelly, I am Heathcliff'.*

10  ***Wuthering Heights** is a novel of passion and revenge. Overall, it is dominated by one character who reacted to all the bad treatment he himself suffered. The fact that the story ends shortly after his death shows his importance. Heathcliff grew to be a demonic figure. However, his relationship with Cathy and Hareton show the reader that he is not entirely evil. He is the main force in the story, making some characters feel like they are in Heaven and others feel like they are in Hell.*

GRADE A1

P = 18/18

C = 18/18

L = 18/18

M = 6/6

Total = 60/60

## EXAMINER'S COMMENT

Good overview in the first paragraph, introducing the main approach within the essay. Some awareness of the novelist's purpose (paragraphs 2 and 4) and there are a number of comments about the reader's reactions to Heathcliff's developing character. Overall, paragraphs are well planned and deal with specific aspects of Heathcliff's influence in driving the story. Reference is wide-ranging and quotations are skilfully used. While the expression is a little repetitive in places, it is competent throughout.

## CHECKLIST

Look again at the sample essay on *Wuthering Heights*.

- are the title and author identified?
- are words from the question used?
- are the aspects intended for discussion in the rest of the essay mentioned?
- are details and examples avoided?
- is a general overview of the question given?

## TASKS

1   Read quickly through the sample answer again and underline the topic sentence in each paragraph. This will help you to focus on the planning of a question. (Note that a good paragraph should follow the pattern **PDQ – Point, Discuss, Quote.**)

2   Read paragraph 8 in the sample answer. Write out the **topic sentence**. Then write out the quote that supports the student's view. (Note how the student discusses the point that Heathcliff is Cathy's hero. We are told that we see a different side to Heathcliff, that he treats Cathy in a special way, that their love story grips the reader's attention.)

## ASSIGNMENT

Now take the sample question and insert your set text and main character into the question:

**Everything that happens in the text, ........., is centred on the character of ........ Discuss this view, supporting the points you make by quotation from and reference to the text.**

(Spend 60 minutes writing your essay.)

## EXAM TIP

- when writing a literary essay, always **make sure that your plan develops a consistent point of view** or argument

- first sentences are important. If possible, **begin paragraphs with a topic sentence** relating the content of that paragraph to your overall theme or point of view in the essay

- **avoid slang,** colloquialisms and contractions (e.g. 'he's' or 'they've' for 'he is or 'they have') wherever possible

- there is no correct length for an essay. Just **use the allocated time carefully,** write concisely and avoid padding.

# Questions on Imagery

## SAMPLE ANSWER

'Shakespeare's use of powerful images heightens our experience of the play *King Lear.*'

To what extent would you agree with this view? Support your answer by close reference to Shakespeare's play.

Possible points for consideration: we appreciate what characters experience through various images.

- suffering and violence
- animal imagery
- sights and blindness
- nature and the storm
- clothing and nakedness
- poverty and nothingness.

1   *This statement is very true, there are many powerful images in the play which improves our experience of it. The first image which I find powerful in the play is that of the love test. Cordelia stands up for what she thinks is right and because of this Lear disowns and banishes her.*

> *'I disclaim all parental care.'*

> *'Better thou hadst never been born than thou not have pleased me better.'*

*It is a very powerful image as we see a father disowning the one daughter who truly loved and cared for him.*

2  *Another powerful image in the play is that of the storm. This is an important image in the play as it reflects what is going on in Lear's mind after Goneril and Regan rejected him. It reflects the powerful conflict in Lear's mind and helps us understand what is going on. Examples of powerful imagery are:*

> *'My wits begin to turn.'*

> *'The tempest in my mind.'*

3  *During the storm we see Lear struggle with his thoughts and we see a better, kinder image of Lear coming through. We see a kind image of Lear who cares for others, and who has realised his wrong doings.*

> *'In boy, go first. You houseless poverty.'*

> *'I have taken far too little care of this.'*

4  *One of the most powerful images in the play is that of Gloucester's blinding. It is violent and vulgar, but it makes the play more exciting and dramatic. We cannot believe that a sister of such good Cordelia, could do something so violent and in such a coarse way.*

> *'Pluck out his eyes.'*

> *'Out vile jelly.'*

5  *Gloucester's suicide attempt is another strong image in the play. It too is very dramatic as he wants to end his life, because of his wrongdoing to his son Edgar, who in the play saves him from his suicide attempt. It is a powerful image not only because it is dramatic, but because we are given an image of good when we see Edgar save his father even though Gloucester had disowned him.*

6  *I believe that another powerful image in the play is when Goneril poisons her sister Regan because they both think they love Edmund. I believe that it is a funny image in a way. We see two sisters fight over a man. Yet they are both married. I feel that this image makes the play a bit more exciting and humorous.*

7  *To me the most powerful image in the play is that of Lear carrying his dead daughter in his arms. It is an image of great sadness as you see Lear's love for his daughter and his regret of lost time. It is a very strong and powerful image in that it brings emotion to the surface.*

> *'My poor fool is hanged.'*

8   *Without these powerful images King Lear would be a fairly dull play, so powerful images do heighten our experience of King Lear. Even though some are not as powerful as others, they still add excitement to the play.*

GRADE: C3

P = 10/18

C = 9/18

L = 9/18

M = 5/6

Total = 33/60

## EXAMINER'S COMMENT

Paragraphs are too short to allow for much discussion or development of points. The style lacks variety and little use is made of quotations, some of which are inaccurate. However, the answer does refer to a range of powerful imagery, and in some cases (paragraphs 4, 5 and 6), there is some mention of the dramatic effects of certain memorable images.

## TASKS

1   The essay style above is repetitive. Write down three alternatives to the adjective 'powerful' (paragraph 2) and three alternatives for the verb 'see' (paragraph 3).

2   Which paragraph do you think is most effective? Briefly list the reasons why.

## ASSIGNMENT

'Striking imagery and symbolism are vital to the playwright's purpose.'

With reference to the Single Text play you are studying, write a timed practice essay (60 minutes) in response to this statement.

**EXAM TIP**

When you are responding to drama answers, it is usually better to talk about the **audience,** rather than the readers of the play. After all, plays are written to be performed and watched by an audience.

However, there are times when it is appropriate to mention the reader. 'Reading' a play can mean interpreting the text and taking meaning from it. It is always worth making the distinction between audience and readers clear when answering Single Text Drama questions.

# CHAPTER 17
# THE COMPARATIVE STUDY

There are a number of **modes** or ways of comparing the texts you have studied. A particular mode allows you to make connections between stories in a focused manner.

There are usually three prescribed modes each year and two of these will appear on the examination paper.

Mode categories include:

- cultural context
- literary genre
- theme or issue
- the general vision and viewpoint.

All these modes of comparison overlap: for example, themes (such as relationships, power, conflict and change) are also aspects of cultural context. However, the modes still offer **separate approaches** to discussing texts. It is very important to keep answers focused within whichever mode you have chosen. Remember that Comparative Study will raise your awareness of fictional worlds and help you understand your own.

# Cultural Context

Every text is set in its own time and place. The author has created a new reality, a particular 'world' or society with its own characters and values. Things to think about include:

- where and when is the story **set**?
- is the **society** free or oppressed? Are individuals free? Are people happy?
- how do people socialise? What **customs** and **pastimes** are popular?
- what attitudes and **values** are evident? What do people consider important and worthwhile?
- how much **conflict** exists in this world? Is racism or nationalism present?
- who has **power** and authority? How do we know?
- what is **family life** like? Consider the role of men, women and children
- are **class** divisions important in this society? What are the author's views about class?
- other influences might well include **religion, superstition, education, money, materialism, marriage, politics, media, changing trends** etc.

# Literary Genre

This refers to the type of text you have studied and how the story is told.

- is **the text** a novel, play, film, autobiography or biography?
- who tells the story? Is it told in a **first person** narrative by one all-knowing (or omniscient) character? Or in a **third person** narrative? How does the narration affect our sympathies and the way we react to the story?

- are we given any hints (**foreshadowing**) about what will happen?
- what about the **structure and organisation** of the story? Is it presented in chronological order from beginning to end? Are there flashbacks or other experiments used in telling the story?
- how are **characters** presented and developed?
- are stage directions or **film techniques** (locations, camera angles, sound, lighting etc.) effective?
- are there any important **images or symbols** used in the story?

The literary genre chosen by the author shapes the narrative and determines our reaction to the story. A brief close-up of a character on the screen can give an insight that would be expressed in a very different way by a novelist.

In comparing texts, it will always be necessary to use supporting evidence. For example, you can refer to memorable moments when the narrator clearly influences the reader's reaction. There may be other key scenes or flashbacks that also make an impact on our understanding of the story. Point out similarities and differences in the ways authors influence us.

# Theme or Issue

Authors explore a great variety of ideas in their work. What is interesting is the different ways in which a particular theme is presented and addressed by writers and film-makers. Modern texts tend to treat themes in a more realistic way, sometimes taking a negative view of human experience. By contrast, happier endings are often found in much pre-twentieth-century fiction.

All the main themes associated with Single Text study are also common in this section. These include:

- love/friendship/loneliness/alienation
- power/corruption/hypocrisy
- conflict/violence
- relationships (personal, with society, etc.)
- change/success/failure
- injustice/racism/nationalism
- comedy/absurdity
- ambition/hatred/pride/loyalty
- family/fate/identity/escape.

# General Vision or Viewpoint

This term refers to the **broad outlook** of the authors of the texts, the main characters and the reaction of the readers or audience.

Texts will have either **optimistic** or **pessimistic** views of life. Sometimes there is a more **realistic**, balanced outlook.

- the subject matter or narrative shape reveals a particular vision of life
- books and films raise questions, and sometimes resolve them
- most texts have features which contribute to their unique atmosphere or impact
- the endings of stories usually leave a lasting impression.

Useful ways to discuss vision/viewpoint:

- comment on the coherence of the viewpoint presented
- highlight the author's attitude towards society
- the author's portrayal of cruelty may illustrate a dislike of such behaviour
- some central characters are morally responsible and do not take the easy way out
- an author might draw directly on his own personal experience
- the hero/heroine may face a moral dilemma
- the author might successfully illustrate how complex life can be.

The viewpoint is pessimistic or tragic because:

- the plot focuses on suffering and failure
- the author's views are bitter and cynical
- the view of women is negative in a patriarchal society
- the use of detached language adds to the pessimism.

An optimistic outlook can be reflected by:

- the resilience of characters who have developed and matured
- some sense of redemption at the end; friendships endure.

The reader/audience may interpret the text as being balanced and realistic:

- the future may not be bleak for every character
- death is a release for some characters
- comic moments compensate for some of the unhappiness
- we are given a realistic insight into a particular time and place
- lyrical/descriptive language adds beauty
- the ending may be very moving, ambiguous or uncertain.

# Guidelines

- it might seem obvious, but remember to take the comparative approach throughout by making **links** between the various texts being discussed

- it is not enough merely to point out similarities or differences between characters or events in different texts. Examiners will expect you to explore **how** authors treat themes, **portray** cultural backgrounds, **present** viewpoints and **shape** stories

- while it is not necessary to study comparative texts intensively, you will need to know main characters and important scenes well to use as illustrations

- avoid drifting into writing summaries of stories when discussing the texts on your comparative course.

## LITERARY GENRE: SAMPLE ANSWER

'Literary genre is critical to our understanding and appreciation of texts.'

**Compare and contrast the different approaches taken in two or more of the texts studied as part of your comparative course.**

*King Lear* – W. Shakespeare

*Things Fall Apart* – C. Achebe

*Witness* – P. Weir

1   *Literary genre is the way a story is told. Each writer is different. We all know that if two people tell you the same story, they will put it across in different ways – just by tone of voice or the gestures they use. It is the same with a novel or a film. Each author or film director puts his or her own stamp on the story. Each one is different in how they tell their story.*

2   ***King Lear*** *is a tragic drama. It tells the main story of a foolish old king who does not really know any of his three daughters well. Cordelia is the only one who really loves her father. We see key episodes in the downfall of this foolish old man from the start when he does a love test to see 'which of you will I say loves me the most?' In dramatic scenes like this, we can understand and appreciate the conflict going on.*

3   *This tragic play is completely centred on one main character, Lear himself. There are a number of dramatic scenes from the 'love test' onwards. For example, where the loyal Kent is put in the stocks and the two older sisters, Goneril and Regan, banish their father. Then there is the madness of Lear with Poor Tom and the Fool. This is also the same in* ***Things Fall Apart***. *There is one main character, Okonkwo. He is the centre of the story. It is told*

139

*in third person narrative which is different to the play. There are episodes or key moments showing how Ibo life used to be. At the end, the white Christians change this. The beginning and end are contrasted. We can appreciate what happened to make such a change to Africa's traditions.*

4 *The book is also divided into three parts. Part I deals with the old Ibo way of life, their rituals, feasts and everyday habits e.g. cooking etc. Part 2 is the exile of Okonkwo and Part 3 is the climax of the story when Okonkwo goes back to his village and cannot cope with all the changes, so he hangs himself. This three-way division lets us compare all the changes that have happened to the traditional people. By the end of the book, white Christians are in Africa and Okonkwo's old ways are disappearing. This three-way division is like* **King Lear** *where there are episodes and key scenes showing Lear's tragic downfall. Lear changes completely and goes through a stage of madness on the heath. Then he is happy for a short while when he makes up with his youngest daughter, Cordelia. But after she is killed, he dies broken-hearted. This is the climax. There is also a climax in* **Things Fall Apart** *in which Okonkwo commits suicide. The two stories show stages of change very well.*

5 *There is also a sub-plot in* **King Lear**. *This is the story of Gloucester, another loyal lord, who is very like Lear. He makes the same mistakes, only with his sons, as Lear does with his daughters. The sub-plot adds to the whole idea of the tragedy because it adds emphasis. We are told the same story twice. This does not happen in the novel* **Things Fall Apart**. *The story concentrates on Okonkwo and we can understand and appreciate his way of life changing.*

6 *Although this is also a tragic story like* **King Lear**, *Okonkwo is an unlucky man who is accidentally banished from his African village for seven years. By the time he returns home, the white missionaries have begun to take over and he kills himself in despair. There is no sub-plot in* **Things Fall Apart**. *We just really see Okomkwo's story on its own. In a way, this makes us concentrate on it more.*

7 *The two stories have symbols to show good and evil. Lear's youngest daughter, Cordelia, is a symbol of goodness. 'Unlike my two sisters who say they love you all, I can't heave my heart into my mouth.' There are also symbols used in* **Things Fall Apart**. *The way the Ibo villagers speak is simple, a symbol of their culture. Even Okonkwo's suicide is a symbol of the end of his country's traditional way of life. This is like Cordelia's death at the end of* **King Lear**. *Both of these tragic heroes have nothing left to live for.*

8 *The story in the film* **Witness** *is more modern and told in a completely different way. The film is about a young Amish community boy who witnesses a brutal murder in Philadelphia. John Book is the detective who investigates the crime and he ends up hiding out with the Amish people. There is a contrast between*

*the modern city life and the old-fashioned traditional Amish life all through the film. This is very like the contrast between white missionaries and Africans in* **Things Fall Apart**. *The city is noisy and violent. Even the police chief is corrupt. Because it is a film, the characters are larger than life on the screen. We can appreciate and understand them on the screen. We can see and hear the people rushing around the modern city. Equally so, the pace of life in the Amish country is very slow. Book just can't fit in. There is one scene where John Book is squeezing into the old-fashioned clothes of an Amish man. As a symbol, this proves how he feels so uncomfortable in the Amish country. Even the music shows the peaceful life of the Amish people who are a caring community who work together in the traditional style.*

9  *The literary genre is critical to our understanding and appreciation of these three stories. They are told in different ways but they are all suited to their stories.* **King Lear** *is a tragic drama about one main character's downfall,* **Things Fall Apart** *is a third-party narrative which explains the way Africa has changed and* **Witness** *is a modern film showing two different sides to life in America.*

GRADE: B3

P = 17/21

C = 15/21

L = 13/21

M = 6/7

Total = 51/70

## EXAMINER'S COMMENTS

A reasonably strong answer which tries hard to remain focused on how authors shape their stories – and strong points are made concisely in paragraphs 4 and 7. There is also a sustained attempt to draw comparisons between the texts. The awkward expression, repetition and inaccurate quotation all take away from the answer. Overall, however, there is a good grasp of how different genres enhance the appreciation of a narrative.

## TASKS

1  'Literary genre' is defined in the first paragraph. Write your own definition, adding anything you think should be included.

2  Go through the sample essay to find where links (similarities or differences) between texts have been made.

## ASSIGNMENT

With reference to the texts you are currently studying for the comparative course, write a timed essay (no more than 70 minutes) in response to the statement: 'Literary genre is critical to our understanding and appreciation of texts.'

## THEME OR ISSUE: SAMPLE ANSWER

'Most texts succeed in exploring important human themes.'

**Discuss this statement in relation to at least two texts you have studied for your comparative course. Your answer must focus on one theme or issue.**

1 *One of the most important issues explored in the three texts I have studied is that of isolation and loneliness. Different aspects and degrees of isolation are dealt with in* **Of Mice and Men** *(John Steinbeck),* **Cinema Paradiso** *(Giuseppe Tornatore) and* **Silas Marner** *(George Eliot). This basic human theme is treated sensitively and honestly in all three texts, and they offer varying degrees of redemption.*

2 **Silas Marner** *offers one of the most acute examples of self-inflicted isolation through the behaviour of the novel's main character, Silas himself. Following his betrayal by his friends, William Dane and Sarah at Lantern Yard, he tried to protect himself in the only way he knew how – by retreating into his own cocoon in the village of Raveloe. After losing all faith in God and man, Silas immersed himself in a solitary world of work, gold coins and alienation. George Eliot presents us with a character who wastes his life because of his deep disappointment. However, she clearly shows us his unhappiness as he works in a routine way every day, avoiding contact with other people and suspicious of the kindness of his neighbour, Dolly Winthrop.*

3 *In contrast with this,* **Of Mice and Men** *successfully explores how loneliness can exist even if a person is not physically isolated. John Steinbeck's novel uses stereotyping to show a variety of lonely characters who are in contact but who are still extremely lonely. Lennie is the retarded adult in a simple world of his own. George is his worried protector. Everyone else on the ranch where they work is isolated. Candy is an old ranch worker, terrified of old age. Crooks is the handicapped servant, the minority black man who is isolated because of racial prejudice. Curley's new wife is trapped in a loveless marriage and desperate for attention. In all these cases, the author keeps highlighting how loneliness brings unhappiness and broken dreams. Only Lennie and George have a close friendship, but it is also far from perfect. Both authors, Steinbeck and Eliot, show how circumstances and bad luck can lead to unfulfilled and lonely lives. All these characters are victims.*

4   *In both narratives, characters feel that the world is against them. In the scene in Crooks' room, Steinbeck symbolises the isolation of Lennie, Crooks, Candy and Curley's wife. All of them speak about their hopes and dreams. Lennie lives for the day when he and George will have a small farm of their own where he will get to tend the rabbits. Candy is also desperate to retire with some dignity. Even Crooks is caught up in the fantasy – until he remembers that it will never be possible because of his racial background. It is interesting that all these characters seem to be unaware of each other as they speak. Curley's wife is filled with regret and bitterness. For years she has been tricked and abused by men. Overall, the level of isolation is deeper and more disturbing in* **Of Mice and Men** *than in* **Silas Marner** *where Silas is able to block out his past to some extent. Unfortunately for Steinbeck's tragic characters, they will never escape their lonely lives.*

5   *The theme of isolation is less obvious in the film* **Cinema Paradiso**. *The story traces the friendship between Toto and Alfredo, a relationship not unlike that of Lennie and George.* **Cinema Paradiso** *is different from the other two texts in that it takes a much more positive approach to relationships. Although characters suffer from loneliness at times, there is a strong community in the small Sicilian town of Giancaldo where Toto grows up helping Alfredo to operate the film projector. It is only when Alfredo advises Toto to go away from Sicily and become successful that we see the loneliness of growing up and leaving childhood behind. There is one touching scene on the quayside where Toto listens carefully to his old friend. This is their goodbye. In the background are anchors that remind the audience of the importance of keeping memories in their rightful place. Although Toto will miss Alfredo and his old home, he will learn to deal with his loneliness in time.*

6   *All three narratives leave us with different degrees of redemption in the end.* **Silas Marner** *is like a fairy-tale in that the arrival of Eppie into Silas's lonely life changes everything for the better. It is obvious that George Eliot is reminding us of the power of love in overcoming isolation and unhappiness. From the moment Silas first sees the golden-haired child replacing his pile of gold coins on the floor of his isolated cottage, we know that redemption is possible. The years spent rearing his adopted daughter humanise the old miser and bring him back to God and the local community. The story is not completely unrealistic, however, in that Eppie's mother, an unfortunate drug addict, dies a cold and lonely life while making her way to confront Eppie's father, Squire Godfrey Cass. Once again, the author is telling readers that luck plays an important role in human affairs. In some cases, loneliness destroys life, but at other times, it can be overcome. Such a balanced view is not present, however, in* **Of Mice and Men**.

7    *In Steinbeck's dark story, most characters attain no redemption whatsoever. After an unfortunate misunderstanding with Lennie, Curley's wife is tragically strangled. This brings an end to any dreams for George, Lennie and Candy. George is finally faced with his worst nightmare and is then forced to shoot Lennie in a heartbreaking mercy killing. In the final scene alongside the beautiful Salinas River, George allows Lennie a final moment of fantasy before his death. We know that he has no choice but to kill his friend before Curley arrives. The story ends by focusing on George's lonely future. From now on, he will be living without someone to 'look out for' just like all the other lonely ranch workers who roam the country looking for casual jobs. This pessimistic ending is in total contrast to* **Silas Marner** *where the central character has overcome his isolation and conquered loneliness. By comparing both texts, we can understand the way fate plays such a part in people's lives.*

8    *At the end of* **Cinema Paradiso***, the grown-up and successful Toto is also able to come to terms with his lonely life away from his childhood home. Although he has regrets, his visit back to Sicily for the funeral of Alfredo allows him a chance to face up to his past. Alfredo has left him a film reel of censored scenes from the old movies they used to show in the years after the war. As he watches the short romantic film clips of couples kissing, we see a shot of Toto smiling slightly. He seems to be thinking of the innocence and wonder of his childhood when Alfredo and the movies brought happiness to his life. Of all the texts, perhaps* **Cinema Paradiso** *leaves us with a balanced view of the way people usually come to terms with loss and loneliness, and generally cope with the realities of life.*

9    *In studying the three texts on the comparative course, we get a much wider view of how different authors appreciate the theme of loneliness and isolation. The three texts are set in very different worlds, but it is clear that human nature does not change very much. Everyone seems to suffer from loneliness to some extent. It is also obvious that isolation brings deep unhappiness and most characters struggle to cope with loneliness – some being luckier than others. Fate and circumstances play a huge role in the lives of all the main characters. From our point of view, we learn more about the wide variety of experiences people can go through – and the devastating effects of loneliness on people's lives.*

GRADE: A1

P = 21/21

C = 21/21

L = 21/21

M = 7/7

Total = 70/70

## EXAMINER'S COMMENT

This is a highly competent and informed response, which showed a clear understanding of how the theme of loneliness was treated in different texts. A strong comparative approach was taken and paragraphs were well organised to explore aspects of the theme in an assured way. One or two more references to key scenes would have been welcome, but the answer was generally very well controlled. There was clear, confident expression throughout and both the introduction and conclusion were insightful.

## TASKS

1   Read the essay very carefully, checking each paragraph in turn to make a list of when direct comparisons are made between two or more texts. Briefly summarise all of the links that have been established.

2   Look for two examples of paragraphs where the candidate could have added an illustration (a key scene or key moment) that would have helped the answer. In each case, give a brief explanation of how the answer would have been improved.

## ASSIGNMENT

With reference to the texts you are currently studying for the Comparative course, write a timed essay (no more than 70 minutes) in response to the statement:

'Most texts succeed in exploring important human themes.'

# Vary the Links

All main Comparative answers need to establish clear links between the texts you have studied. Useful phrases to point out similarities and differences between texts are:

- in a similar way ...
- by contrast ...
- this is not the case in ...
- in a slightly different way ...
- on the other hand ...
- this is not unlike ...

## EXAM TIP

Avoid repeating titles.

Abbreviating titles can produce a disjointed note-like answer. It's better to avoid repetition of titles by referring to them in different ways. For example:

- *Pride and Prejudice*: Austen's narrative/story/world/text; the nineteenth-century novel
- *Dancing at Lughnasa*: the Donegal story/drama/tale/text; Friel's play/story
- *Strictly Ballroom*: Luhrman's film/world; the Australian story/text.

## GENERAL VISION AND VIEWPOINT: SAMPLE ANSWER

'Vision and viewpoint can vary greatly from one text to another.'

**In the light of the above statement, compare the different approaches taken in the texts you have studied as part of your comparative course.**

*The three texts I have studied are:*

1 *Pride and Prejudice by Jane Austen*
2 *Dancing at Lughnasa by Brian Friel*
3 *Strictly Ballroom directed by Baz Luhrman*

1 *The most famous quotation in **Pride and Prejudice** is the opening sentence: 'It is a truth universally acknowledged that a single man in possession of a good fortune must be in want of a wife.' We realise straightaway that Jane Austen, who is writing about her contemporary society, is immediately mocking it. Similarly, Baz Luhrman in **Strictly Ballroom** is mocking and ridiculing the strict rules and pressures found in the competitive world of Australian dance schools. They both realise the flaws of their two different societies and openly laugh at them. In contrast to these two texts, Brian Friel is looking back on the problems of Irish society during the 1930s.*

2 *In **Pride and Prejudice**, Jane Austen shows readers her views through the central character of Elizabeth Bennet, the second eldest of the five sisters. Jane Austen makes it clear that she is laughing at the idea that people should marry mainly for money. In particular she ridicules the character of Mrs Bennet whose first reaction when she hears of a wealthy young man, Mr Bingley, arriving in the neighbourhood, immediately thinks of him 'marrying one of our girls'. Although Brian Friel is writing about a very different world, he also presents*

*marriage as the key to a better life for women in the Ireland of the 1930s. None of the Mundy sisters is married and Chris was the only one who got a proposal from Gerry Evans – who as it turned out was already married. In* **Strictly Ballroom**, *the only marriage we see is between Doug and Shirley Hastings. It doesn't seem to be much of a marriage of love – until the end when they dance together. Baz Luhrman depicts Australian women as self-absorbed and false. Similarly, in* **Pride and Prejudice**, *Austen shows Mrs Bennet to be a typically domineering housewife who is only interested in her daughters marrying well. Luhrman also shows Shirley Hastings, Scott's mother, in a very bad light, as domineering and pushy.*

3  *All three authors refer to dancing to further show their general vision and viewpoint. In* **Strictly Ballroom**, *it is the main theme of the film, and the relationships between characters are explained through the dancing. Similarly, in* **Pride and Prejudice**, *it was at dances that members of the opposite sex got to meet each other. Jane and Mr Bingley met at a dance, and the relationship between Mr Darcy and Elizabeth started at a dance when he was too proud to ask her to dance – 'she is only tolerable – not handsome enough to tempt me'. This started her prejudice against him. Similarly, the relationship between Fran and Scott is explored through dancing in* **Strictly Ballroom**. *At the beginning, Scott ignores Fran and she calls him a 'gutless wonder' when he refuses to dance with her. This reminds us of the time when Darcy insulted Elizabeth in* **Pride and Prejudice**. *Both these texts are also about the pressures on young women.*

4  *Friel explores the anxieties and frustrations of the five Mundy girls. One of the best examples of their pent-up feelings is the scene when they dance together in the kitchen of their home. The wild release they get from dancing like children is a sign of their inner frustration – 'I want to go to the dance, Kate. I don't care how sweaty or how drunk they are. I want to dance.' At this point, Agnes seems to realise that she isn't as old as she sometimes feels. For once she admits the truth that she wants to dance and enjoy herself because it is the festival of Lughnasa.*

5  *Dancing is a form of release in Friel's story, but Luhrman portrays dancing as challenging and rigid in* **Strictly Ballroom** *where non-federation steps are not allowed. In contrast, dancing is a very formal part of the social lives of* **Pride and Prejudice**. *Like everything else in that world, young ladies are dressed up and on show on such occasions. This is a long way from the wellingtons and worn clothes that the women in Donegal wear, but when the Mundy sisters dance, they dance in a natural way as if the dance frees them.*

6 *It is clear that Jane Austen sympathises with Elizabeth Bennet about the importance of love as the basis for a true marriage. Elizabeth is slightly shocked when Charlotte Lucas remarks that 'Happiness in marriage is a matter of chance' and that it is 'important to know as little as possible about the defects of the person with whom you are about to pass your life.' Baz Luhrman seems to have a similar view on love when he tells the story of the romance between Scott and Fran.*

7 *By contrast, Friel really lets us see the trap that women can find themselves in trying to find happiness and security. He makes it clear that a loving marriage is the ideal situation, but this is a risk. Irish women take a chance on marriage. The alternative of living a lonely life can also be bad. Friel himself had two aunts like Rose and Agnes who ended up destitute and alone. I think that his outlook on life was influenced by their experience.*

8 *All three texts have similarities and differences in their general vision and viewpoint because the three authors have their own unique views of life. Overall, they seem to be telling us that luck plays a great part in whether or not people are happy and fulfilled. Elizabeth Bennet was fortunate that she found love and security. Scott and Fran were also lucky to find each other. The Mundy sisters have a much tougher time and their future is not so good.*

GRADE: A2

P = 19/21

C = 17/21

L = 17/21

M = 7/7

Total = 60/70

## EXAMINER'S COMMENT

Although a little note-like, this is a well-written answer that avoids a common error of focusing only on the endings of stories. Some paragraphs (paragraph 4, for example) drift close to being mere summary and lose sight of the question. There is a confident approach throughout and clear links are made between the texts. The concluding paragraphs are effective and offer a good overview.

## TASKS

1 Read through this essay again, picking out the places where vision or viewpoint are referred to (either explicitly or implicitly).

2 Use one key quotation from the ending of a comparative text on your course that clearly highlights the final vision and viewpoint expressed in the text.

## ASSIGNMENT

With reference to the texts you are currently studying for the comparative course, write a timed essay (no more than 70 minutes) in response to the statement:

'Vision and viewpoint can vary greatly from one text to another.'

> **EXAM TIP**
>
> When writing about texts, avoid awkward expressions such as 'It says in the novel ...' Think of alternatives, such as 'We learn that ...' or 'The author lets us know ...'

## CHAPTER 18
# PRESCRIBED POETRY

# Writing Successful Poetry Answers

Keep in mind that the examiner will expect evidence that you have engaged directly with the poems themselves, so:

- reflect on both the poet's themes and his/her interests
- comment on the poet's characteristic style and viewpoint
- give your own personal opinion backed up with evidence.

## EXAM TIP

In addition to making general comments about themes and style, it is good to focus on two or three key poems in some detail. You may also refer to the poet's own life and how his/her experiences shaped particular poems.

Avoid relying entirely on prepared poetry notes. Your own personal response will be well rewarded. It is important to show that you have engaged with the poetry.

Pay close attention to the task you have been given in the question. For example, are you writing a letter to one of the poets? Are you giving a talk about a particular poet? Perhaps you have been asked to write a newspaper article, a review, or an introduction to a new collection of the poet's work. Organise the layout of your writing as required and make sure that you use the appropriate tone. This will make your work convincing and give it an authentic feel.

# Eavan Boland

## SAMPLE ANSWER

**Write an essay on the poetry of Eavan Boland, explaining how you responded to the poems you studied. Support the points you make by reference to or quotation from the poems on your course.**

Possible points for consideration:

- the major themes and issues explored in her work
- the poet's own life and influences
- how you yourself related to particular poems
- her vision and humanity
- poetic style – language and imagery.

1   *When I first read the poem 'Child of Our Time', I thought there was something very gentle about the way it was written. At the same time, Eavan Boland was dealing with a very disturbing subject. When I found out about the background to the poem and that she wrote it after seeing a newspaper picture of a child who was killed in an explosion, I saw Eavan Boland as a very emotional woman who had great sympathy for innocent victims. Other poems, such as 'The Famine Road' and 'The War Horse' also show great understanding of suffering.*

2 *What I like most about the Eavan Boland poems I have read is her quiet way of expressing herself. Her style of writing seems like a lullaby. Boland is able to express a number of different feelings. Apart form being sorry for the young child in 'Child of Our Time', she also attacks the way politicians and terrorists and the ordinary citizens of Ireland are all responsible in one way or another for the death. She says 'we must learn from you dead'. Not only is she condemning violence, she is also hoping that the death will have made people change their minds. It is also interesting to see that Ireland has become more peaceful in the last few years, partly on account of similar bombings, such as Omagh. These also shocked people.*

3 *'The Famine Road' shows Boland's interest in Irish history. Again, the reason I really liked this poem was because of the human approach the poet took. The poem was not filled with a lot of facts and figures about the potato famine. Instead of this, the poet gives us the different voices of actual people involved at the time. In the first stanza, we hear the heartless voice of someone in authority who was in charge of famine relief. As far as he is concerned, the Irish are lazy and 'as idle as trout'. The tone of voice is cruel as if the ordinary people are not even human. The sentence 'their bones need toil' gives us a shocking picture of their hungry bodies and the inhuman way they are being treated by those in authority.*

4 *In some ways, 'The Famine Road' is very like a drama with different characters speaking their parts. I found this a more interesting way of imagining the famine from the point of view of those involved back then. We also hear another speaker in the third stanza, the voice of Boland herself. The stanza contains many disturbing pictures of the horror of the famine when the starving peasants were so desperate that they even thought about cannibalism. Some of the dramatic images are almost unreal to us today, such as when the poet describes how some people were almost driven mad by hunger, so that they even considered other humans as food: 'each eyed – as if at a corner butcher – the other's buttock'.*

5 *At the end, Boland brings the poem up to date and links the suffering of the famine with the way some women today are treated by doctors who ignore their feelings as individuals. I thought this was a very good way of showing that those in authority can still talk down to ordinary people, in this case a woman who cannot have a child. The doctor dismisses her in an inhuman tone, 'grow your garden, keep house'. What the poet says to me is that people are still powerless and ignored in life. They may not be starving but they are desperate.*

6 *I also found 'The War Horse' to be very moving and had a powerful theme about the way so many people retreat behind the privacy of their own homes and ignore what is happening outside. The poem begins with an ordinary story about a runaway horse that is wandering through a suburban estate. But even the title makes us think of a deeper meaning. The horse is a symbol*

*of violence and also our fear of it. The poet uses language that reminds us of how horses were once part of warfare. There are many images of suffering, such as 'a maimed limb', 'corpses' and 'the screamless dead'. Boland paints a picture of the people inside their safe houses as selfish, not interested in the violence going on in the outer world or in the past. They can do nothing about the situation except look after themselves, 'we are safe'. I think this is a very honest poem, since most of us just look out for ourselves and don't want to really get involved with the trouble others are going through. Although Boland appears gentle in her tone, there is great strength beneath what she is saying and this is something that made an impression on me.*

7  *Overall, the poem I liked best by Eavan Boland was 'The Black Lace Fan My Mother Gave Me.' I think this was because it told a story and showed the realty of a love affair. The poem is about the courtship of the poet's parents when her father gave her mother this special gift of a black lace fan. I liked the opening describing the hesitant way they behaved on one of their first dates:*

> *'She was always early.*
>
> *He was late. That evening he was later.*
>
> *She ordered more coffee. She stood up.'*

*The short phrases suggest the tension between the couple and this kind of thing still goes on when lovers are unsure about each other. Everyone is on edge and this comes through in the language. To me, the fan represents the mystery between couples, and the way love changes over time. Yet love lasts, just as the fan itself has lasted. I like the way the poet celebrates the love between her parents. It is sad also because the souvenir of the fan is a reminder that nothing lasts forever.*

8  *In conclusion, I would say that I enjoyed reading all the poems of Eavan Boland. To me she is a poet who writes about real events and takes a very emotional approach. Her themes and subjects are ordinary ones but are interesting. She involves the reader in her poems by making us think of how we react to such subjects as Irish history, violence and love. Her soft-sounding language does not mean that her feelings are not very strong in her poems, and I liked this very much.*

GRADE: A1

P = 15/15

C = 15/15

L = 15/15

M = 5/5

Total = 50/50

## EXAMINER'S COMMENT

This is a very well-written answer which shows a clear understanding of Eavan Boland's work. There is a sustained thoughtful approach throughout. The response is positive and appreciative without being gushing. Although there are few quotations, they are apt and integrated well into the critical comments. 'The Famine Road' is dealt with very effectively and in some detail over several paragraphs. All in all, an insightful and competent response.

## TASKS

1   Read through the essay again and find five sentences (or phrases) that show a personal response to the poet. Write down the five examples. (The second sentence in Paragraph 3 might be one.)

2   Leaving aside the introduction and conclusion, the essay includes six paragraphs. Starting with Paragraph 2, write down the main point (or central idea) of each paragraph. (For example, you could say that Paragraph 4 highlights how 'The Famine Road' is dramatic and shocking.)

3   List the summary points that are included in the final paragraph of the essay.

## ASSIGNMENT

Choose one of the poets on your course and write a personal response to the poems you have studied. (Allow yourself about 50 minutes to plan and complete the essay.)

Use the Eavan Boland essay as a guide to help you plan main points that are well supported with reference and quotation from the poems.

# John Donne

## SAMPLE ANSWER

**Does the poetry of John Donne still have appeal to the modern reader? Support the points you make by detailed reference to the poems on your course.**

Possible points for consideration:

- the poet's unique views on love, religion and death
- his dramatic power and directness
- ingenious treatment of themes and eccentric reasoning

- his varied tone and casual, conversational style
- the variety and freshness of his imagery
- his use of argument and logic
- his metaphysical wit – using paradoxes, puns and conceits.

1   *The poetry of John Donne is extremely interesting, exciting and witty, and although it was written during the Renaissance, it is still relevant today. This is one of the reasons why one should read Donne's poems. John Donne is one of the leading metaphysical poets, a group that dealt with complex themes, such as the relationship between God and man, lover and beloved as well as time. Whether addressing his lover or his God, Donne always uses a confident tone.*

2   *Donne finds images for his poetry in a number of very  unlikely sources, including science, astrology and astronomy, and this makes his poems even more interesting. There is a brash and over-confident male voice found in his poems – just like  actual speech. There are so many fresh ideas that it is easy to recommend his work to anyone interested in literature.*

3   *In 'The Flea', Donne tries to persuade his loved one to become intimate with him. He asks her to consider 'how little' is the thing that she denies him. Donne pleads with his love and uses the argument that the flea has already sucked her blood without loving her. It has also sucked his blood, so both of them have already 'mingled'. Donne also says: 'And in this flea, our two bloods mingled be'. He argues that the flea's sucking of her blood has done no harm to her and that she should therefore give in to him without 'sinne, or shame, or losse of maidenhead'.*

4   *In the second stanza, the poet adds to his argument by using outrageous logic. Donne is sacrilegious when he says that it is as if they are in the body of the flea: 'O stay three lives in one flea spare'. This is a startling parallel to the Holy Trinity and so Donne risks blasphemy. He goes even further when he uses a conceit to describe the flea and compares its body to a beautiful, exotic, black stone: 'And cloistered in this living wall of jet'. This statement is extremely startling since a cloister was a sacred place where laypeople were not allowed to enter. Yet Donne describes how he and his love are united within it.*

5   *In the third stanza, Donne takes on a mock heroic tone when he talks about how his love has killed the flea. He argues that by killing it, she did not hurt herself or lose any honour. He then ingeniously goes on to turn the argument around and says that if she allows herself to be his lover, she will not be weakened in any form. It will not be 'a sinne nor shame'. These kind of arguments are typical of Donne and makes it compelling reading as it is witty, clever and humorous.*

6   *I believe that Donne's poetry is full of fresh and exciting imagery and arguments that are still relevant today. In 'Batter My Heart', he pleads with God to reform him because he is a sinner and is taken with the material things in life. The poem opens with a dramatic order to God: 'Batter my heart, three personed God'. The poem is full of violent and fiery imagery to convey how Donne needs to become better and this makes for ripping reading. Through the use of these images, the poet accuses God of being too gentle with him in the past, but now he pleads with God to reform him and 'break, blow, burn and make me new'. The use of violent and exciting verbs adds excitement and the run-on lines throughout the poem conveys movement and energy.*

7   *Donne also uses paradoxes in the poem, such as when he demands that God destroy him so as to 'make me new'. These unusual images make the poem more interesting and worth reading. He compares himself to a 'usurpt town' that has been taken over by God's enemy. Donne wants to be loyal to God, but he is tied 'unto the enemy'. He startlingly imagines himself as a woman and God's lover and he needs God to rescue him. The poem closes with another paradox: 'nor ever chaste except you ravish me'. Donne is sure that his soul will not be saved.*

8   *Donne's poem 'The Anniversarie' is of interest because it deals with love in such an unusual way. He talks about the growth and continuity of love. The poem starts with a list, but it is given in order to belittle:*

   *'All kings, and all their favourites*

   *All glory of honours, beauties, wits,*

   *The sun itself.'*

   *Donne was very critical of the public time and of the court, since he and his wife had suffered because of the intrigue of the court. In this poem, he also deals with the themes of love and eternity. He believes that the love between himself and his wife will last forever. He uses a conceit of two royal people to show how their love is everlasting.*

9   *In 'A Valediction Forbidding Mourning', Donne uses mathematical images to convey his love for his wife and how they will never be parted. He compares her to the fixed foot of the compass and he is the arm that moves around.*

10  *Donne's poetry is extremely relevant to today, whether it is a young man courting a woman or a man pleading with God to reform him. Donne's use of arguments, startling parallels, conceits and paradoxes all make his poetry compelling reading.*

GRADE: C1

P = 10/15

C = 9/15

L = 10/15

M = 5/5

Total = 34/50

## EXAMINER'S COMMENT

While the answer contains general note-like comments about Donne's poems, few of the paragraphs focus directly on showing how his themes are relevant today. At times, the question seems to have been forgotten – in paragraphs 5 and 9, for example. At the same time, there is an implicit awareness that Donne is a compelling poet whose fresh approach is highlighted. Expression is awkward in places and repetition is also a problem, with overuse of some adjectives, e.g. 'startling'.

## TASKS

1   Paragraphs 4 and 6 could be improved by varying the expression and avoiding repetition. Write out both paragraphs again, making sure that the writing is more varied and interesting.

2   Which of the paragraphs in this sample answer do you consider is the most effective as a response to the question? Explain why it is successful.

## ASSIGNMENT

Choose one of the poets on your course and write a timed answer (50 minutes) in response to the same question as the sample on John Donne.

## EXAM TIP

When writing about a poet's **style**, don't simply list features such as alliteration or repetition. There's no point in saying that a writer uses sound effects or a metaphor without some details and explanation of how these things create meaning and feeling.

# Michael Longley

## SAMPLE ANSWER

Write a short essay on the aspects of Michael Longley's poems (their content and/or style) that you found most interesting. Support your discussion by reference to or quotation from the poems you have studied.

Possible points for consideration:

- the range of themes in his poetry
- the relevance of the poems to the modern reader
- the poet's descriptive powers and eye for detail
- his humanity and sensitivity to people and events
- the relationships he explores
- the freshness and honesty of his point of view
- humour and pathos
- his language, imagery, rhythms and tone.

1   *The majority of Longley's poems deal with his relationship with his father and references to violence. His father served during the war and Longley was brought up in Northern Ireland. This accounts for his preoccupation with violence.*

2   *It is apparent that he had a very close relationship with his father. He shows this when he talks of the two memories from his father's head – 'kept like secrets until now'. This shows the trust and intimacy between them in the poem 'Wounds'. When his father is dying he says tenderly 'his thin head I touched.' In the poem 'Laertes' he shows a son's will to throw his arms around his old father and cry 'and blurt out the whole story.' It is a very loving poem displaying great respect and love of his father.*

3   *In the poem 'Last Requests' we see Longley's need to reach out and comfort his father. His father cries out for a Woodbine cigarette but Longley has only brought peppermints and grapes. He feels inadequate and helpless. He wishes he could grant his father his wish.*

4   *Longley's poems are also very preoccupied with violence. His poems remind us a lot of the situation in Northern Ireland; the senselessness and ugliness of violence.*

5   *The poem 'Wreaths' deals with a young IRA man entering a civil servant's home. The man was going about his daily routine in the privacy of his own home 'preparing an Ulster fry for his breakfast.' The IRA man shot him with no remorse. 'To his children, to a bewildered wife, I think, sorry missus was what he said.' This shows the horrors of violence and killing where an innocent man was shot down purely for his religious beliefs. It is shocking and a very effective poem.*

6   *Longley likes to shock his readers. He highlights the senselessness of the violence and the devastating effects it can have. He talks about the greengrocer 'serving even the killers'. Both references here have shown a human touch – where above the killer says 'sorry missus' and where the killers pay for the groceries. It is as if they have no problem with the person they have killed but what they stand for. Whereas Longley tries to show us that the victims were in fact just ordinary, decent people.*

7   *Longley further stresses the ugliness and lack of pride involved in violence in the North in his poem 'Ceasefire'. 'Bellies full of Irish beer, flies undone.' When he makes reference to the state the killers were in when they were lured into being killed.*

8   *Longley's poems are very interesting and consistent in their content. The style of his poems is effective too. He uses shocking images and says the message bluntly. Longley is honest with the readers and is not trying to glamorise fighting in the North. He writes about it the way it is. The language he uses is accessible and the theme is clear. A clear message is being put across in each poem.*

9   *Longley writes about the personal and often with a subjective slant. One could argue that he just presents facts, but I believe that he holds a certain bias. I believe he is anti-war and anti-violence. I believe the main purpose of Longley's poems is to persuade, to convince and to shock.*

*(550 words)*

GRADE: C2

P = 10/15

C = 9/15

L = 8/15

M = 4/5

Total = 31/50

## EXAMINER'S COMMENT

While paragraphs 2, 8 and 9 made good points and were well supported by quotation, the shorter paragraphs (e.g. 4 and 7) were noticeably lacking in any worthwhile development. There was also scope for much more in the way of personal response and engagement with the material. The answer would be expected to focus on the appeal of Longley's poetry. Overall, the expression could have been more controlled and varied.

## TASKS

1   In your view, what could be added to paragraph 4 to improve it?
2   Find one example of where a quotation is used (a) very effectively as part of a longer sentence; and (b) less effectively because it is not placed in context.

## ASSIGNMENT

Write a timed essay (50 minutes) about the work of a poet on your course that really impressed you. Make detailed reference to at least three of the poems.

## EXAM TIP

Plan paragraphs so that they deal with particular aspects of the poetry that you find interesting. Keep the emphasis on why the poems appeal to you. Deal with both content and style of writing. Perhaps you have shared some of the poet's feelings or experiences. Avoid starting answers with a prepared biography of the poet. Details about the poet's life are better used when discussing particular poems and how these were shaped by the poet's experiences. Finally, use reference and short quotations effectively to illustrate key points.

## ASSIGNMENT

Write a timed essay (50 minutes) in which you discuss the relevance of one poet whose work you have studied as part of your poetry course. Support the points you make by close reference to the poems you choose to write about.

## EXAM TIP

When composing your essay answers, remember to:

- **keep to your plan.** Once you've started writing, keep to the structure of main points (in paragraphs) that you have planned
- **lead readers through.** Disjointed or jumbled writing will not be rewarded
- **keep your ideas flowing.** You can do this by using such simple but important linking words as: although, but, therefore, and, as a result, thus, however, consequently, moreover, whilst, which, although, yet
- **write fluently.** Lead the reader smoothly through your writing, controlling the pace and linking points together
- **come to a conclusion.** The ending says a lot about how well you have organised your answer – and it's often what stays longest in the reader's memory. The final paragraph should leave your audience knowing your main ideas or point of view.

# Responding Personally

Although most poetry questions are likely to ask for a **personal response**, you might well be asked to take a particular approach, such as giving a talk about the poet or writing an introduction to the poet's work.

These are some more typical poetry questions:

History and tradition are central themes in the poetry of _____. Discuss etc.

If you had to select four poems by _____, which would you pick and why?

While most of the poems written by _____ are autobiographical, they have a universal significance. Would you agree with this view? Give reasons etc.

The poetry of _____ is enjoyable for a variety of reasons. Discuss etc.

If you were giving a public reading of some poems by _____, which ones would you choose? Give reasons etc.

# Poetry – Relevant or What?

Another fairly common question concerns the relevance of a poet on your course, for example:

**Does the poetry of a particular poet have still appeal to the modern reader?**

## EXAM TIP

In planning a response to such a question, think about the following points:

- are the poet's ideas rebellious or controversial?
- which of the poems still have meaning today?
- are the poet's concerns still of interest or in the news?
- is he/she in conflict with authority?
- do you understand and relate to the poems?
- did you find the poet's life particularly interesting?
- were you sympathetic to him/her?
- were you impressed by the energy or feeling in the poems?
- is the poet's use of language original or striking?

# USEFUL WEBSITES

## www.bbc.co.uk/education/

A wide-ranging site, providing lots of ideas to improve writing skills.

## www.skoool.ie

Includes interactive Leaving Cert English coursework and education news.

## www.historychannel.com/speeches/

Listen to famous speeches from history and learn about persuasive language.

## www.bartleby.com

An astonishing collection of resources are gathered together on this Columbia University website. For a start, its own encyclopaedia, the Columbia Encyclopaedia, is well worth consulting. Also available here are online editions of many plays, novels and poems; reference books such as a dictionary, a thesaurus and books of quotations; and guides to the rules of grammar and writing style. This may be the closest the Internet has yet come to providing a full library on one website.

## www.powa.org/

This website styles itself an 'online writing assistant' and it's really very good. In particular, click through to the informal, argumentative and exploratory essay sections.

## http://landow.stg.brown.edu/victorian/victov.html

The Brown University Victorian website contains detailed material on all aspects of the work of Charles Dickens. Social and political history, gender matters and other topics are covered in the treatment of such notables as Charlotte Brontë and Thomas Hardy.

## http://tlc.ai.org/shakespe.htm

The Teaching and Learning Centre, Indiana, provides a comprehensive guide to the works of William Shakespeare, with a rich list of links to study material on all of his plays. Essays, lesson plans, theatre directions and more are presented in a classified format.

## www.sparknotes.com

There is a large collection of substantial revision notes here on literary texts – a summary, an analysis of characters and themes, questions, etc.

## www.scoilenet.ie

Includes guidelines and notes on the English course.

*Good luck with your studies!*

# Acknowledgments

The author and publisher are grateful to the following for permission to reproduce copyrighted material:

Article by Margaret Driscoll copyright: NI Syndication first published in *The Sunday Times*, 18 April 2004;

Diary entry by Dr Clare O'Leary first published in *Ireland on Sunday*, 23 May 2004 reproduced courtesy of *Ireland on Sunday*;

Interview with Damon Wayans by David Coombs first published in *The Funday Times* Issue 764, 1 January 2004 courtesy of *The Sunday Times*;

Reviews of *Mission Impossible* and *The Haunted Mansion* first published in *Hot Press*, 25 February 2004, vol. 28;

'How to Survive the Leaving' first published in *Face Up Magazine*, September 2003 reproduced courtesy of *Face Up Magazine*;

'The Cult of Celebrity' reproduced by permission of Oxford University Press from 'The Cult of Celebrity' from *New Headway Advanced Student's Book* by John and Liz Soars;

'Bully For You' was written by Brenda Finegan, Editor of GATE (God And Time Embrace) Magazine, which is an alternative youth magazine, distributed to schools throughout Ireland. The first issue was produced in January 2000 as a millennium project in the Archdiocese of Armagh, and the magazine was officially launched by Archbishop Sean Brady in September 2003 as part of The Strategic Plan of the Armagh Diocesan Youth Ministry. Rev. Gerard Campbell is Chairman of the GATE Editorial Board. Contact GATE at www.gatemagazine.com.

Speech by Trevor Sargent T.D. first given at the Galway Ard Fheis in March 2004 reproduced by kind permission of Trevor Sargent T.D. Leader/Ceannaire, Green Party/Comhaontas Glas;

Extract from *A Kestrel for a Knave* by Barry Hines (Michael Joseph, 1968) Copyright © Barry Hines, 1968 Reproduced by permission of Penguin Books Ltd.;

Extract from *Livewire* by Martina Murphy reproduced by kind permission of Poolbeg Press Ltd.;

Extracts from 'Shadows' by Gwen Devins. Shortlisted for the Sunday Tribune Hennessy Literary Award 2004. Copyright © Gwen Devins 2004. Gwen is a new Irish writer in the process of completing her first novel;